a complete guide to learning
THE IRISH FIDDLE

by PAUL McNEVIN

Copyright © 1998 Walton Manufacturing Ltd.
2-5 North Frederick Street, Dublin 1, Ireland

All rights reserved including the right of reproduction in whole or part
in any form or by any electronic or mechanical means including any
information storage or retrieval systems without prior permission in writing
from the publishers except for a reviewer who may quote brief passages.

Transcriptions and Engraving • Gregory Magee
Cover Design • Temple of Design
Editor • Pat Conway
Cover Photograph • Neil MacDougald
Photographs • Ena Doocey

Order No. WM 1319
ISBN No. 1-857200845

Exclusive Distributors:
Walton Manufacturing Co. Ltd., 2-5 Nth Frederick Street, Dublin 1, Ireland.
Walton Music Inc., 494 Saw Mill River Road, Yonkers, New York 10701

Printed in Ireland by ColourBooks Ltd.

Contents

Introduction	5
Parts of the Fiddle	6
The Bow, Strings, etc.	7
Holding the Fiddle	8
Holding the Bow	9
Finger Positions	10
Music Theory (1)	12
Bowing and Counting Ex.1 & 2	13
Music Theory (2)	14
Sharps & Flats, Accidentals and Scales	16
Ex. 3, 4 & 5	17
Double Bar Lines & Time Signatures	19
Merrily We Roll Along Ex.6	20
German Polka Ex.7	21
An tSean Bhean Bhocht Ex.8	22
Fáinne Geal an Lae Ex.9	22
The Kerry Polka Ex.10	23
The Three Note Jig Ex.11	23
Mo Ghile Mear Ex.12	24
The Britches Full of Stitches Ex.13	24
Terry Teahan's Polka Ex.14	25
Bowing, Bow Strokes and Technique	26
Ex.15-20 Bowing Exercises	27
Ex.21-25 Bowing and Rhythm	28
Ex.26-30 Bowing Fingered Notes	29
Ex.31-38 Slurring	30 - 31
Regional Styles	32 - 35
Ex.39-44 Ornamentation (1) - The Cut	36 - 37
Ex.45-53 Triplets	38 - 39
Ex. 54-67 Rolls	40 - 43
Johnny I hardly Knew ye Ex. 68	44
Maguire's March Ex.69	44
Out in the Ocean Ex.70	45
The Old Favourite Ex.71	46
Garret Barry's Jig Ex.72	47
Ex. 73 - 76	47
Morrison's Jig Ex.77	48
The Hag's Purse Ex.78	49
Ex. 79-80	49
The Cliffs of Moher Ex.81	50
Ex.82-86 Ornamentation (2)	51
Ex.87	52
The Butterfly Ex.8	52
Coleman's Slip Jig Ex.89	53
Thug Mé Rúide Ex.90	53
The Blackhaired Lass Ex.91	53
Ex. 92-93, 95-96	55
The Plains of Boyle Ex.94	55
The Boys of Bluehill Ex.97	56
Off to California Ex.98	56
Alexander's Hornpipe Ex.99	57
Harvest Home Ex.100	57
The Roving Pedlar Ex.101	59
The Orange Rogue Ex.102	60
Port na bPúcaí Ex.103	61
Planxty Irwin Ex.104	62
Bunclody Ex.105	62
Ex.106 Polkas and Slides - Johnny Leary's	63
Duggan's Polka Ex.107	64
Dennis Doody's Ex.108	65
O'Sullivan's Fancy Ex.109	65
Bakerswell Polka No.1 Ex.110	66
Bakerswell Polka No.2 Ex.111	66
The Priest Ex.112	67
Mary Willie's Ex.113	67
This is My Love Do You Like Her? Ex.114	67
Going to the Well for Water Ex.115	68
Kerry Slide No.2 Ex.116	68
Ex.117-119	69
O'Connell's Trip to Parliament Ex.120	69
Jackie Coleman's Ex.121	70
Joe Cooley's Ex.122	71
The Wise Maid Ex.123	71
Jenny's Chickens Ex.124	72
The Morning Dew Ex.125	73
The Pigeon on the Gate Ex.126	74
Ex.127-128	74
Advanced Ornamentation Ex.129-143	75 - 78
Miscellaneous Tunes Ex.144-182	79 - 104
Appendix	105
Discography	106 - 108
Festivals and Events	109 - 110
Bibliography and Further Reading	110

Said the fiddle to the warpipes, 'You're made up of drones
You can boast of but one octave, and you have no semitones',
Said the warpipes to the fiddle, as his eyes now flashed with fire,
'For untruthfulness and impudence you come second to the LYRE -
You mentioned just a while ago about my arms and legs.
But you boast of none at all, for you have only pegs;
And what is more, I say, sir, that your head is only glued,
And anyone can see, sir, that you're very often screwed',
Said the fiddle, 'I've a belly and a back and sides, moreover,
And a shift or two at intervals, my nakedness to cover;
I've a head-piece and a tail-piece, and though I'm often tight,
I've a bridge to rest my bones upon when I retire at night;
My audience I can move to tears, with feelings of emotion,
Without using golden syrup or any other lotion . . .

The Warpipes versus the Fiddle

by John Smithwick Wayland

(from O'Neill's Irish Minstrels and Musicians)

Introduction

The Fiddle, or Violin, as it is known in classical circles, has been pivotal in the development of Irish music. It has existed since the middle of the sixteenth century and has become a potent symbol of expression for the cultures of many countries.

The instrument itself is played by rubbing horse hair (from a horse's tail!) across the four strings, causing the strings and the wood of the fiddle to vibrate. This sounds quite crude and explains the delicate touch needed to play the fiddle – which in turn is perhaps why so many styles, inflections and sounds can be obtained from one instrument alone.

The music itself has been passed on for many years through parents, neighbours and local musicians. The lack of communication and the inability to travel beyond the local community meant isolation and therefore the profusion of many local styles throughout Ireland. Traditional music was more a way of life at the beginning of the twentieth century than it is today. Then came the commercial recordings of the 1920's with the likes of James Morrison and the great Michael Coleman, setting a new standard and providing an opportunity for many local musicians to hear the music from a different perspective. People learned quickly from these recordings and could now choose or copy a style not native to their region. Since then a new generation of musicians has emerged, with some learning more from recordings than from any other source.

The fiddle is one of the most subtle and sensitive instruments and can be immensely rewarding when practice comes to bear fruit. Most good musicians you might see or hear have been inspired to teach themselves. I hope that this book will go some way in doing that for you. Some musicians decide to get involved after hearing an inspiring performance or seeing the social barriers that are broken down through music; others are born into the music and see it as a way of life.

If you find music particularly tough, you might be lacking motivation to practise. It's important to realise that one must practise regularly to become a reasonable player. Some musicians are said to be naturally talented, but in many cases they have been encouraged, heard reams of music and were probably given invaluable hints and tips from their peers. But like everybody else, they had to practise.

I believe that anybody can play music well. It is up to the individual to gather the patience, enthusiasm and the will to practise and develop the art. It is important to involve oneself as much as possible when approaching an instrument. Go to festivals, fleadhs and sessions just to look and listen. Try to learn something each time you hold the instrument. I have provided hints and tips for dealing with the problems you may come across along the way. Also, try to learn 'by ear' as much as possible by listening to other players and recordings. Try to remain relaxed when playing, in order to improvise and express yourself properly. This is a common characteristic of players at the virtuoso level. Above all, enjoy the experience – and persevere.

PAUL MCNEVIN

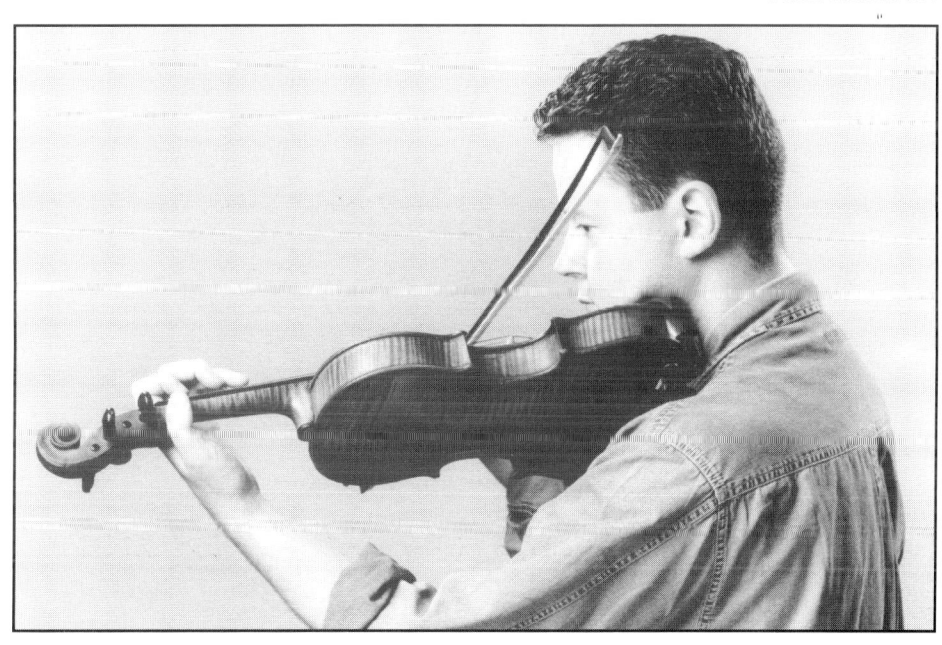

Parts of the Fiddle

A fiddle can contain some seventy individual parts. Here are just a few.

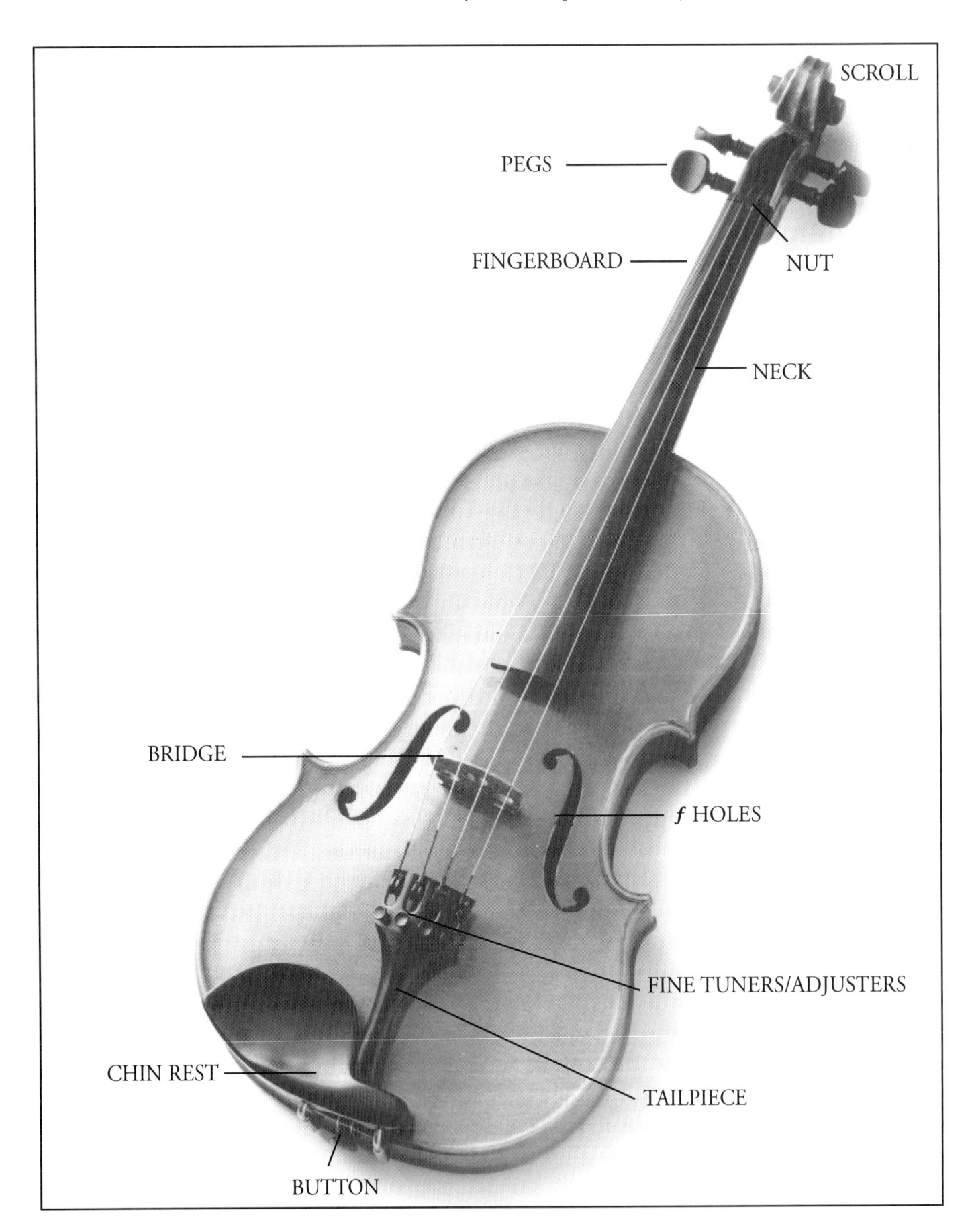

The Bow

The stick of the bow is often made from pernambuco wood. The hair connecting the nut to the tip usually consists of horse hair, although a synthetic hair is sometimes used. Turn the screw clockwise to tighten the bow and keep the hair as clean as possible. The bow should be loosened when put into the case to preserve the springiness of the stick. For more on care of your instrument, fiddle repair and strings, see appendix.

Strings

There are four strings on the fiddle – G, D, A and E. The lowest in pitch is G, on the left side; next is D, followed by A, and the highest in pitch is E. Strings are made of metal, nylon or gut, with metal strings being the most popular for traditional music. Sometimes strings come with a small plastic section. This is placed on the bridge to prevent the coil of the string from unravelling and to stop the string wearing down into the bridge.

Fingerboard

The fingerboard is where the fingers are placed to create a note. The fingers press on the strings until they touch the fingerboard.

Fine Tuners/Adjusters

These are used to fine-tune after the pegs have brought the strings close to the preferred pitch. They are turned clockwise to raise the pitch. Make sure that the adjusters are screwed in firmly to the tailpiece, otherwise, you could hear a buzzing sound when playing.

Pegs

The pegs are used to keep the tension at the scroll end of the fiddle. They are also used for tuning.

IRISH MUSIC
The Instruments

No one really knows what ancient Irish music was like, but its importance to the Gods and consequent magical properties are colourfully described in mythology. In an account of a magic battle between the Tuatha De Danann and the Fomorians, the God Dagda of the Tuatha overcomes his fleeing enemies by means of the harp's three musical feats: the goltraí which causes the host to weep, the geantraí which causes them to burst into laughter, and the suantraí which sends them all to sleep. Though these attributes of the harp are but literary conventions, that a type of harp existed in Ireland at a very early age and occupied a privileged position in the culture seems certain. According to evidence left by stone carvings made before any type documented in Western Europe, it is speculated to have originated in the middle east (possibly Egypt). Certainly the Celts as a people were well established in Central Europe by 500 B.C. providing a flow of civilisations from the East through which an instrument such as the C-shaped cithara might have found its way. In any event, the Irish harp in its present triangular form had emerged by the twelfth century, A.D. as an instrument peculiar to the country and officially recognised as conferring upon its players a special status in society. The ancient harp was quite solidly constructed, with a large, hollow sound box and a deep heavy neck.

Continued on P.15

Holding the Fiddle

The fiddle is placed on your left collarbone and shoulder. The shoulder is pushed upwards, supporting the fiddle. Make sure the fiddle is pushed gently against your neck and that your face is not looking down on the fiddle. As you look, the fiddle should be slightly left of centre. A shoulder pad or rest can be attached underneath the fiddle to support it, giving a more secure grip at the neck and shoulder.

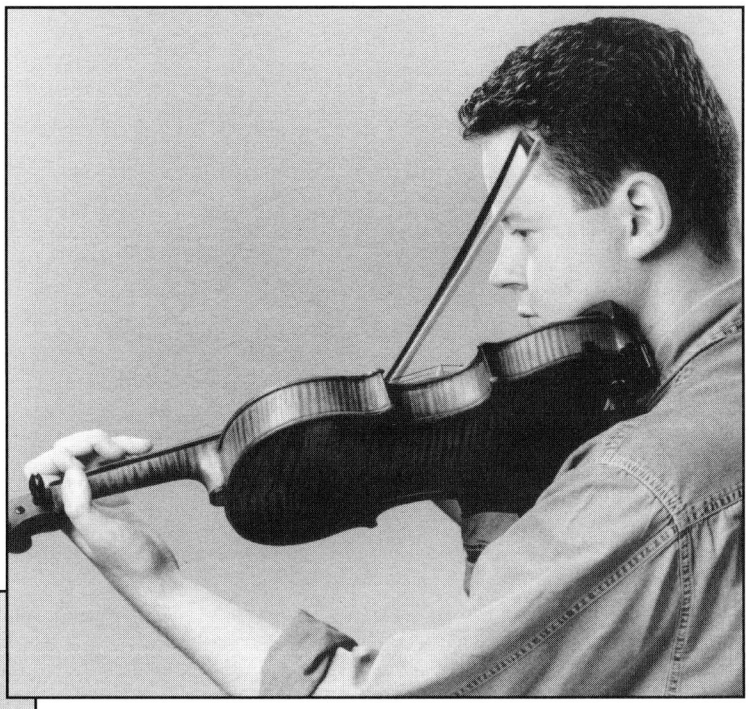

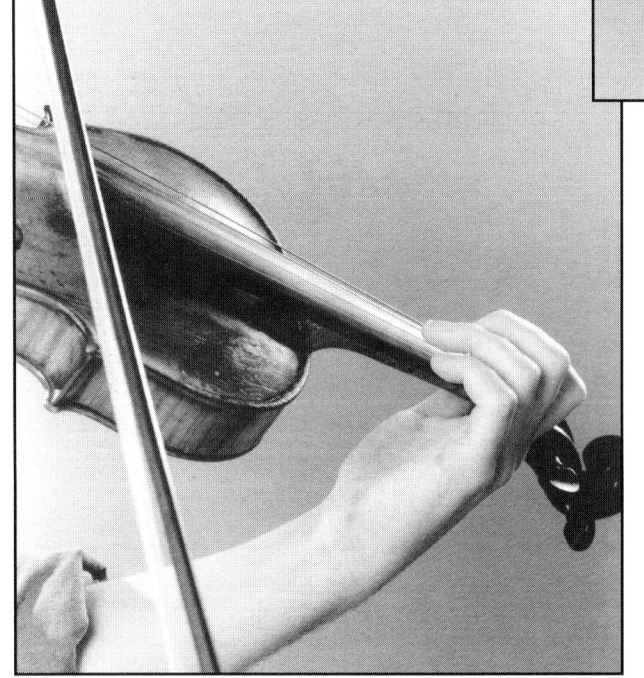

The neck of the fiddle is held lightly between your thumb and first finger. It rests just at the first joint of the thumb and just above the third joint of the first finger. Your wrist underneath the fiddle is kept in line with the elbow so that the palm of the hand is kept away from the neck. Keep your left elbow several inches away from the body and underneath the fiddle. The fingers are arched over and kept close to the fingerboard. The end joints of the fingers should be almost vertically over the strings.

KEY POINTS

Ensure that the fiddle is high enough on your shoulder so that you are not straining to hold it with your neck.

As described above, the fiddle is held under your neck against your shoulder. Don't rely on the use of your hand to support the weight of the instrument. Don't have the fiddle tilted too much at a right angle. This could make bowing on the E string more difficult.

Holding the Bow

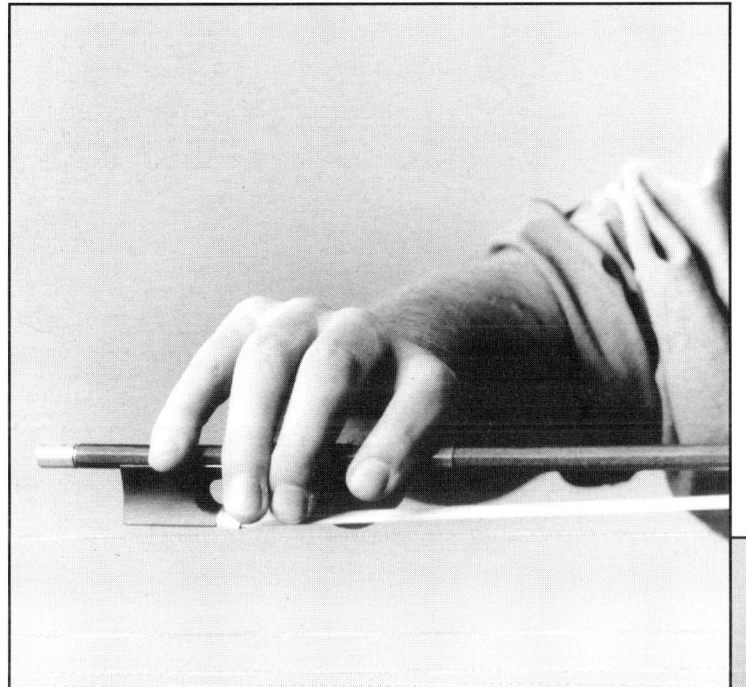

There is no set way of holding the bow in Irish music. It will take time and several minor adjustments to find a hold you are comfortable with. All fingers of the right hand are placed on the bow with the inside line of the first joints of the first three fingers curling around the stick. The first finger controls most of the pressure on the bow. The little finger rests on the stick for balance. It is important to have the wrist twisted in toward you to ease the wrist movement.

You may find it a strain to keep the fourth finger on the bow at all times, so lifting it when playing close to the tip is quite normal. Place your thumb on the black tape above the metal winding just above the nut. This should give you the best balance when using the upper half of the bow. N.B.: With the tip of the thumb on the bow, the thumb knuckle should be bent slightly in order to prevent the hand from tensing up.

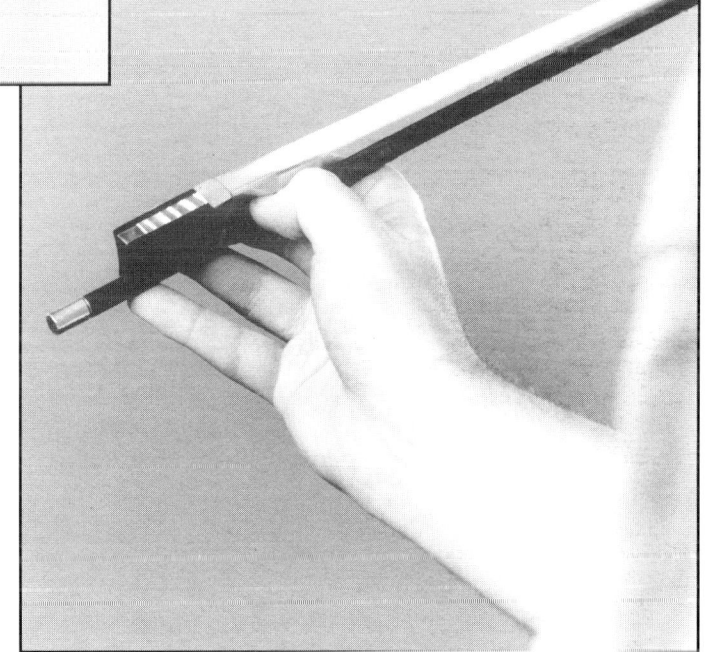

KEY POINTS

The bow hair should never touch the stick at any time but will come close at your heaviest pressure.

Keep the hair roughly 1cm away from the stick at the centre of the bow.

Keep your right elbow quite low. The height of the elbow only changes crossing strings.

To ensure greater accuracy of intonation, make sure the *tips* of the fingers press down on the strings.

Make sure that you are quite relaxed when holding the instrument and that you have a firm grip on the bow.

Finger Positions

Below is a picture of the finger positions as they appear when you look at the fiddle.
Between the first and second finger positions notes are missing. We'll come to them in due time.

(notes on the fingerboard)

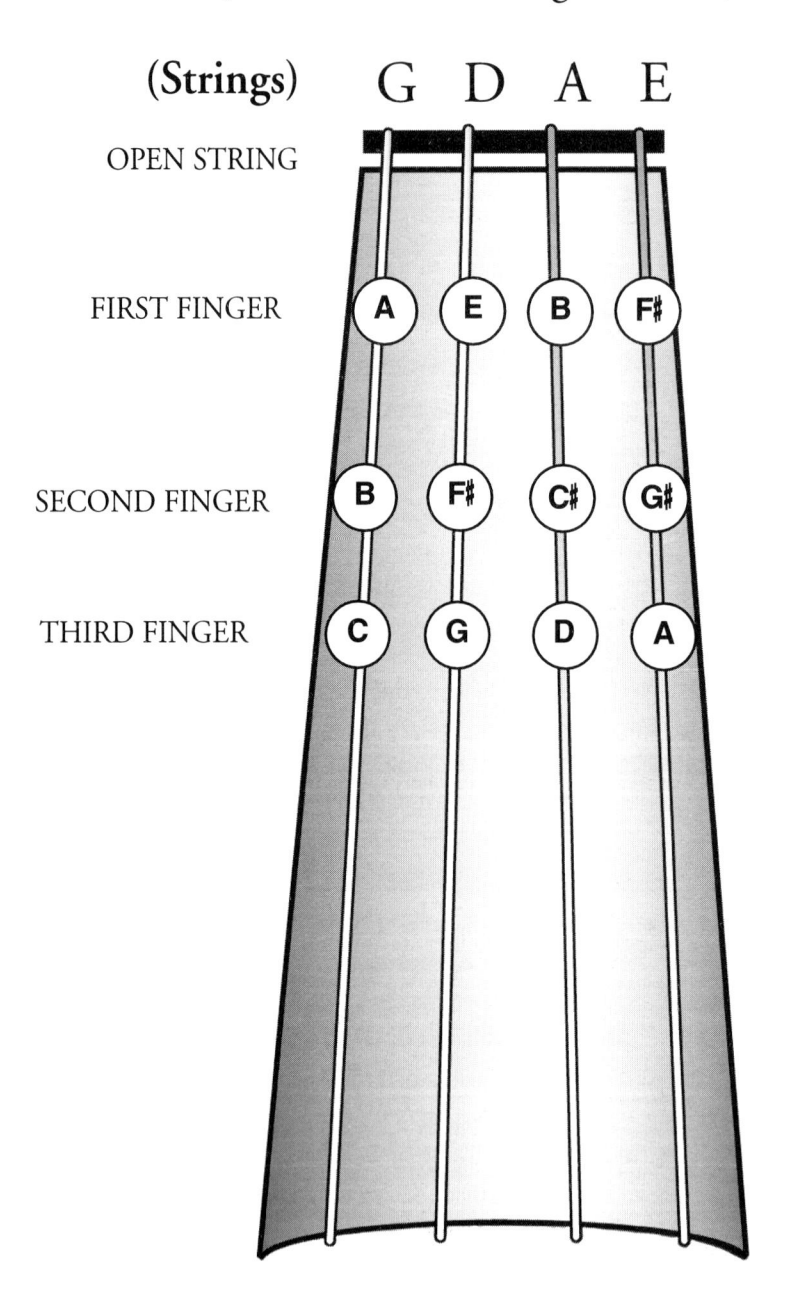

(Strings)	G	D	A	E
OPEN STRING				
FIRST FINGER	A	E	B	F#
SECOND FINGER	B	F#	C#	G#
THIRD FINGER	C	G	D	A

Martin Rochford, Clare

Music Theory (1)

Here is a table of rhythmic values. Each successive note value is worth half of the previous value.

Note symbols have a time value, i.e. they show the duration of the note. The table below shows the most common ones and their corresponding rests. **Rests** are used to denote timed periods of silence in music.

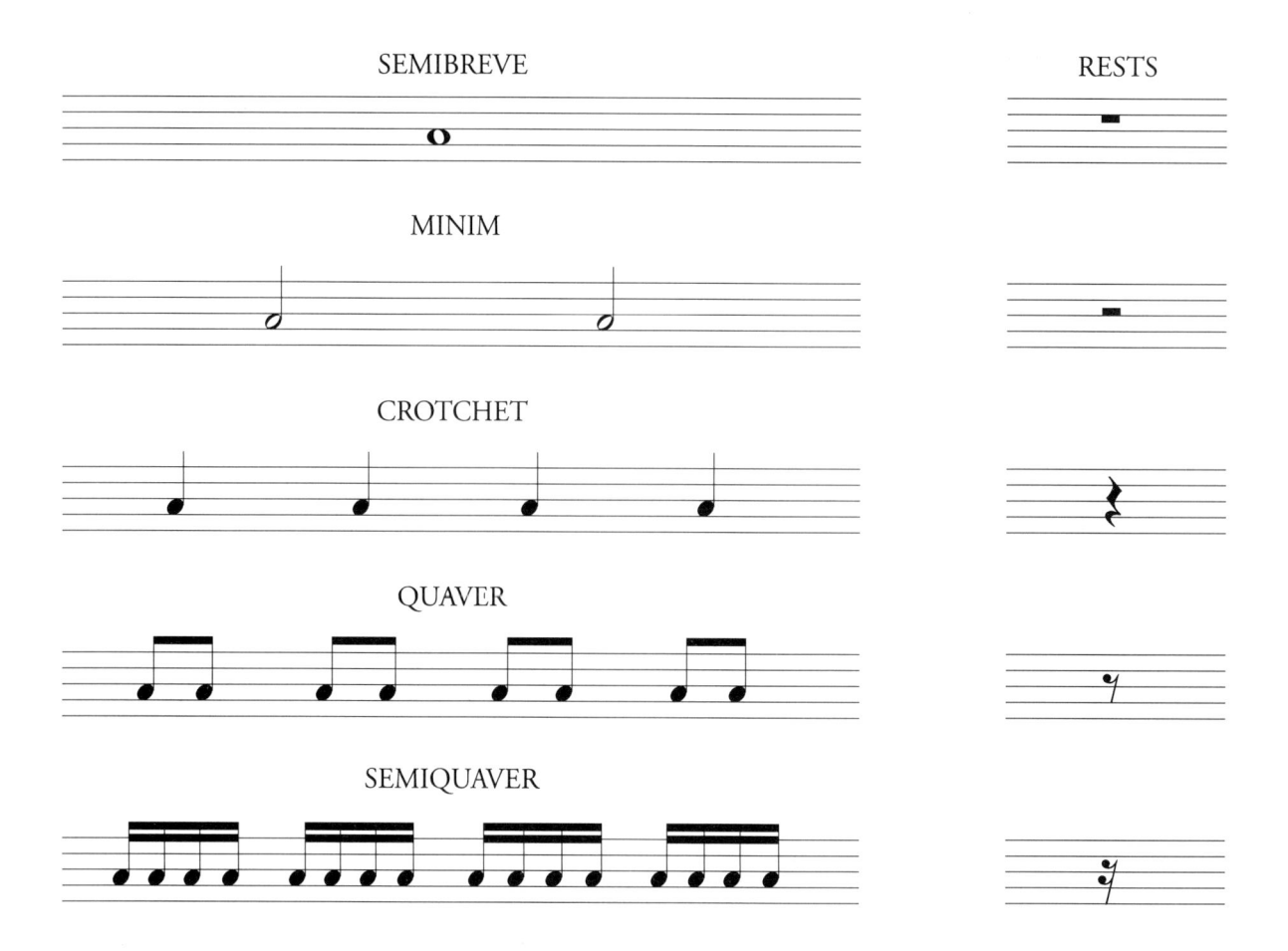

SEMIBREVE   RESTS

MINIM

CROTCHET

QUAVER

SEMIQUAVER

Dotted Notes

A note may be made longer by placing a dot after it. The dot increases the value of the main note by half.

Tied Notes

A tie is a symbol placed above or beneath two notes to indicate sustain for the duration of the two notes, i.e. once the first note is sounded the player holds through till the end of the second. In the example, the crotchet and minim will sound for the length of a dotted minim.

Bars

A tune is divided by a series of vertical lines called **barlines**. A bar refers to the music contained between two of these lines. The emphasis in the music generally falls on the first note of each bar. Most Irish tunes are approximately sixteen bars in length, often consisting of two eight bar sections

Bowing and Counting

Try counting out loud first before playing these two bowing exercises.

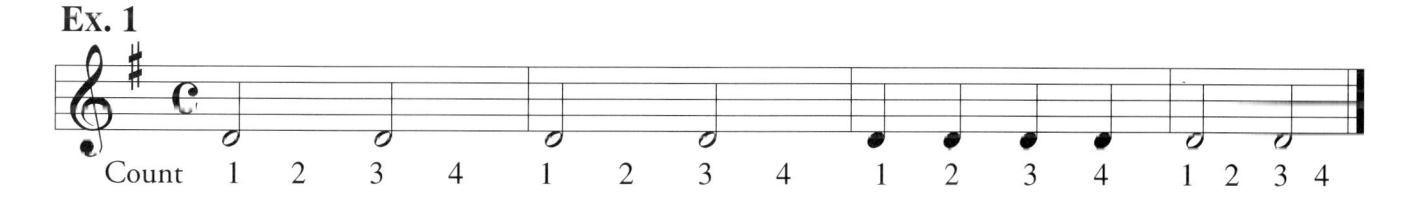

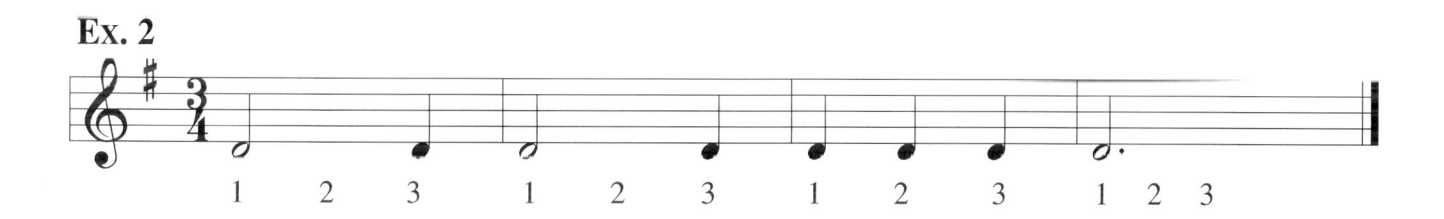

Ex. 1

Count   1 2 3 4   1 2 3 4   1 2 3 4   1 2 3 4

Ex. 2

1 2 3   1 2 3   1 2 3   1 2 3

Music Theory (2)

Musical notes are written on a system of five equally spaced lines called a stave. Their position on the stave denotes their pitch.

The notes are named after the first seven letters of the alphabet - A, B, C, D, E, F, G. In the case of Irish traditional music, a **treble clef** is placed at the beginning of each stave.

This tells us where the general lie of the notes will be, e.g. a **bass clef** is used for lower pitched instruments such as the double bass.

A note is written either on a line or in the space between two lines of the stave.
The notes on the lines of the treble clef are:

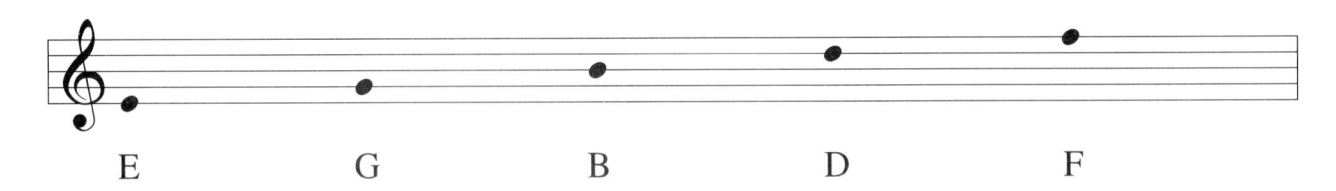

E G B D F

Useful Mnemonic/Memory aid:
"Every Good Boy Deserves Food"

and the notes in the spaces are:

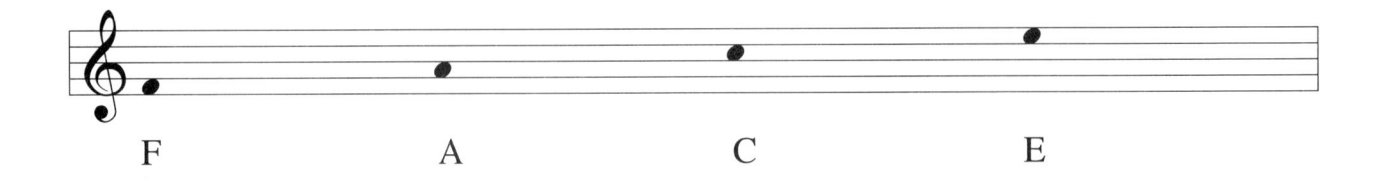

F A C E

Putting the lines and spaces together we get

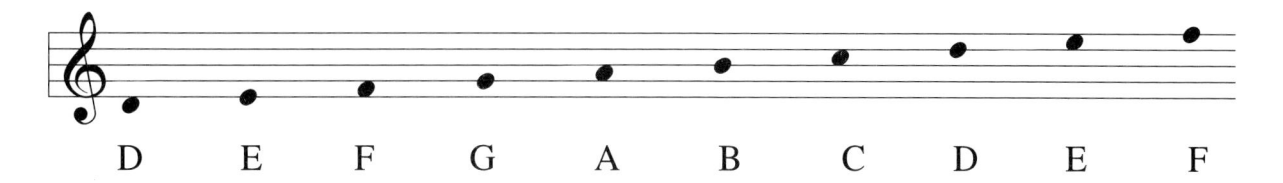

D E F G A B C D E F

Notes which are too high or too low to be placed on the stave are written on short added lines called **ledger** lines which effectively extend the stave upwards or downwards at that point.

Here is a note chart including leger lines, and most of the notes needed to play Irish music.

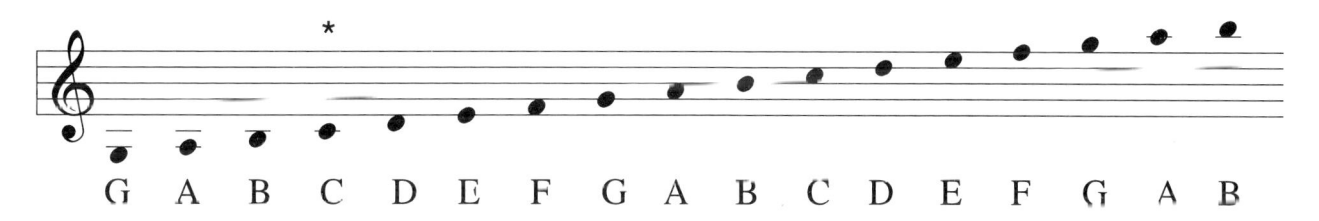

G A B C D E F G A B C D E F G A B

* **Middle C** is so called because it is located at the centre of the piano keyboard.

It is vital to memorise the lines and spaces and their positions on the fingerboard.
Test yourself by turning to any tune later in this book.

IRISH MUSIC The Instruments - continued

Its strings were of thick brass and were played with the fingernails. The oldest existing model is preserved in Trinity College, Dublin and dates from the fourteenth century - one of the few instruments which has survived intact from medieval Europe. Harpers of the period used no system of musical notation and thus the exact style of music in vogue at the time has been lost, but evidence left by the scholar Giraldus Cambrensis at the end of the twelfth century indicate that though refined, the music played was not substantially different to that popular in the courts of Europe. Distinctive to Ireland, however, was the inclusion of harpers at bardic recitations.

Sadly, by the end of the eighteenth century, harpers had lost much of their ancient status and the few survivors of the tradition were mostly blind itinerant musicians. Even the respected Turlough O'Carolan (1670-1738) who has left a legacy of tunes still played today gained a great deal of his credibility through his departure from the pure Irish tradition and his incorporation of Italian and German styles favoured by the gentry. By 1781 the Irish harping tradition was near extinction and following a belated stirring of patriotism, an Irish gentleman resident in Copenhagen instituted the idea of annual meetings or competitions for harpers which were subsidised by the gentry.

Continued on P.25

Sharps and Flats

These are symbols which denote an alteration of certain pitches in a piece of music.

♯   SHARP – this raises the pitch by a semitone (half a note interval)

♭   FLAT – this lowers the pitch by a semitone.

♮   NATURAL – this restores a note to its original pitch after one of the above.

Note: There are also double flats and double sharps, but these do not occur often in Irish music.

A **KEY SIGNATURE** is a sequence of sharps or flats placed at the beginning of a stave, after the clef, which indicate that certain notes throughout that stave will be altered accordingly. Accidentals may also occur within the piece.

Accidentals

Apart from appearing in the key signature, sharps and flats can also occur within a piece. In this case the sharp or flat, referred to now as an accidental, remains in effect to the end of the bar or until otherwise altered by another accidental.

Scales

A major scale is made up of eight notes: **e.g.** C D E F G A B C

The difference between a note and the next nearest note is a semitone. Two semitones make up one tone. For instance, C♯-D and E-F are semitone steps and C-D and E-F♯ are tone steps.

The interval between the third and fourth, seventh and eighth note in any major scale is a semitone; all other intervals are a tone. Therefore, the intervals of a **D scale** are as follows:

1st	2nd	3rd	4th	5th	6th	7th	8th
D	**E**	**F♯**	**G**	**A**	**B**	**C♯**	**D**
TONE	TONE	SEMITONE	TONE	TONE	TONE	SEMITONE	

EXERCISE   Practise the scales described on p. 19 to get used to the finger intonation and shape (relative sharps and /or flats in each scale). Use one bow stroke per note.

Practise each scale both ascending and descending.

The Key of G

In the key of G, all F's are sharpened.

G A B C D E F♯ G

The key of G is indicated at the beginning of the stave by placing the sharp on the F line, i.e.

Ex. 3

The Key of D

The key of D has 2 sharps. All F's and C's are sharpened.

D E F♯ G A B C♯ D

The key of D is indicated at the beginning of the stave by placing a sharp on the F line and C space, i.e.

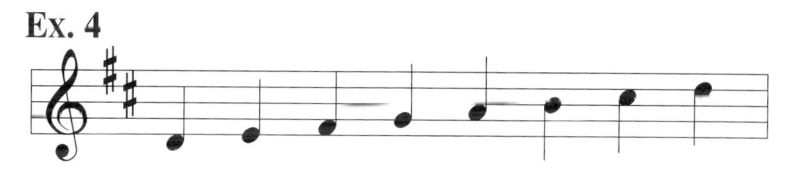

Ex. 4

The Key of A

The scale of A has 3 sharps.

A B C♯ D E F♯ G♯ A

The key of A is indicated at the beginning of the stave by placing a sharp on the F line, C space and G space, i.e.

Ex. 5

The Key of C

The key of C has no sharps or flats in its scale; thus, it has no key signature and would appear as follows:

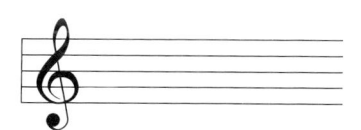

Top: Dónal Ó Mairtín, Michael O'Riordan, Danny Magner
Left: Eileen O'Brien.
Right: James Kelly.

Double Bar Lines

The end of a tune or a section within a tune is indicated by a double bar line (A).
When a double bar line is preceded by two dots (B), this means that the part must be repeated.

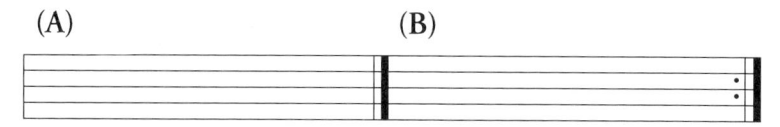

(A) (B)

Time Signature

At the beginning of a tune you will find two numbers placed one above another telling the rhythm and therefore the type of tune. The top number tells you how many beats in each bar, while the bottom number indicates the type of beat, e.g. half note, quarter note, etc.

$$\frac{2}{4} = \frac{\text{The number of beats} = (2)}{\text{Type of beat in a bar} = \text{Crotchet}}$$

Here are most of the time signatures that you are likely to come across:

2/4	Seen mostly in polkas	6/8	Found in jigs and set-dances.
9/8	Seen mostly in slip jigs	12/8	Found in slides

4/4   The most popular time signature, found in reels, hornpipes, marches and most set dances. It is also referred to as **Common Time** and can be indicated by the letter **C**.

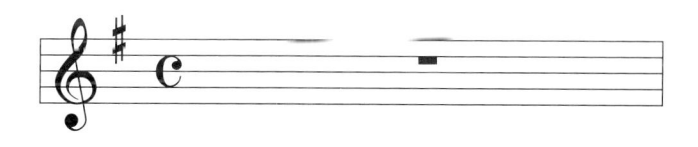

Lets Play Your First Tune

This, your first tune, also has words to help you with the rhythm. If you can sing and play at the same time, your future looks promising! There are only three notes used in this tune, played on the D string, D, E and F. Here are their finger positions:

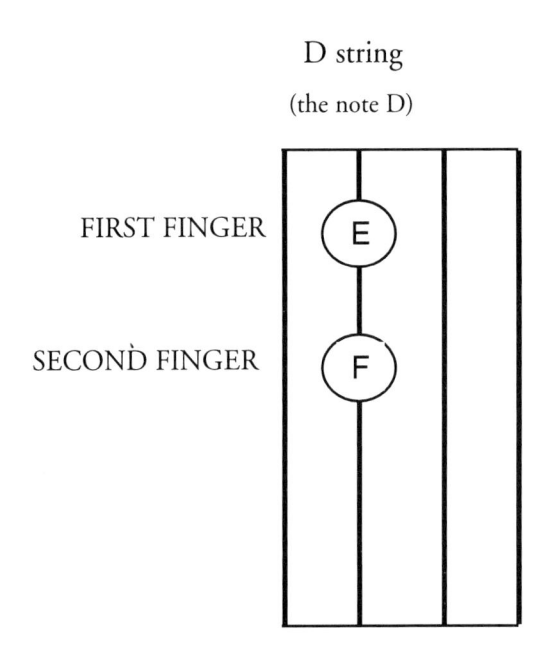

D string

(the note D)

FIRST FINGER — E

SECOND FINGER — F

Merrily We Roll Along

Play long bows for the black notes and very long bows for the white notes.

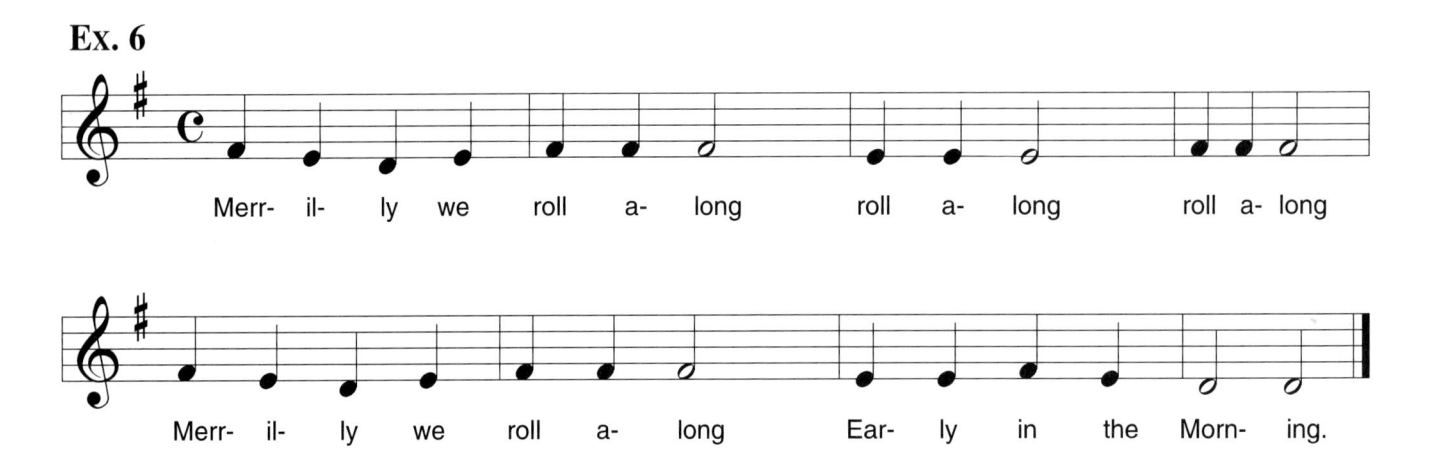

Ex. 6

Merr- il- ly we roll a- long roll a- long roll a- long

Merr- il- ly we roll a- long Ear- ly in the Morn- ing.

German Polka

This is another simple tune that uses five different notes.

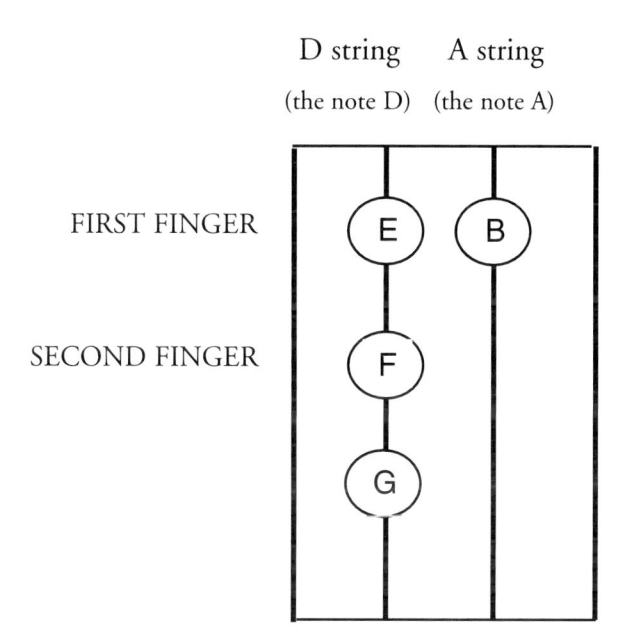

D string   A string

(the note D) (the note A)

FIRST FINGER   E   B

SECOND FINGER   F

G

German Polka

Try to learn this tune off by heart so that you can concentrate more on your technique.
All the notes in this tune are shown above on the fingerboard.

Ex. 7

An tSean Bhean Bhocht

Practise the G scale (starting on the third finger D string) a few times before trying this tune in G. I have some bow strokes added also; try them after you have learned to play the tune with the right rhythm.

Ex. 8 See page 26 for these bow strokes (⊓, V). **Air**

*G natural played with second finger on 1st string close to the first finger.

Fáinne Geal An Lae

When approaching a tune, try to get the air of the tune in your head by listening to the tape. The rhythm of this tune in D is counted immediately after each bar, so tap your foot and follow along the written music while listening to the tape.

Ex. 9 **Air / March**

The Kerry Polka

This is a good beginner tune in D as most of it is played using only the A and E strings. Be careful of the rhythm, though — the dotted notes are longer and the semi-quavers are played quickly, as if they are part of the phrase after them. Again, leave the bow strokes until you are familiar with the tune, then try adding them later.

Ex. 10

The Three Note Jig

Believe it or not, this tune only has three notes. Unfortunately, this is very unusual. It makes it easier to concentrate on the rhythm of the tune, which is a jig — a type of tune very common in sessions.

Ex. 11

Mo Ghile Mear

This tune was originally an old Irish air; it translates well onto the fiddle.
Keep the bows quite long, especially for the minim notes.

Ex. 12 *Air*

The Britches Full Of Stitches

This is a well known polka played in the key of A. Try to learn this and earlier tunes off thoroughly, so that you can concentrate on technique and being relaxed when playing.

Ex. 13 *Polka*

Terry Teahan's

This is a tune that typifies the bounce and rhythm found in Sliabh Luachra music.
Notice how the bowing adds to the flavour of the tune.

Ex. 14   Polka

The Instruments - continued

The first of these meetings took place in Granard, Co. Longford and the idea was later taken up by liberal citizens of Belfast who wished to outdo their Southern neighbours. At the first Belfast Festival of 1792 few entrants submitted themselves for the competition, an indication of the declining state of the art. Of these ten, only one, a 97 year old Derry man named Denis Hempson, played in the true traditional style, with long crooked fingernails upon brass strings.

There were other instruments played in medieval Ireland besides the harp, notably the bone whistle, a two-drone bagpipe and the tympan (a stringed instrument played with a bow), but these instruments were associated with the lower orders and were thus ignored in ancient annals. As early as 1160 an account of the Carman Fair from the Book of Leinster describes the chief entertainments as "bagpipes, fiddles, men of no valour, bone players and whistle blowers". Though the word fiddle was coming into common use, it was not the violin known today, but rather the above described tympan. Nonetheless, a type of fiddle music was evolving concurrently with that of the war pipe.

Continued on P.54

Bowing

The character of Irish music depends more on bowing than on anything else. Various regional styles are distinguished by variations in the bowing. Bowing can affect volume, tone and timing; it gives the distinct rhythm that characterises reels, jigs and hornpipes. No two fiddlers will have the same bowing patterns or have the same technique when bowing. This is especially true of the more experienced players.

Bow Strokes

When the right arm moves away from the fiddle (from nut to point of bow),
the bow stroke is called a **down bow**.
It is indicated by a (∎) sign placed over the note.

When the right arm moves towards the fiddle (from point to nut of bow),
the bow stroke is called an **up bow**. It is indicated by a (V) sign placed over a note.

Technique

Continually revise the holding of the bow and do the bowing exercises regularly. The wrist must remain relaxed so that the angle between the hand and forearm can be constantly adjusted.
The right hand should have a tight enough grip on the bow to be in full control.
The grip on the bow must always remain the same.

It is important to remember that the bow is top-heavy. If the nut (gripped end of bow) is near the strings it will put pressure on the third and fourth fingers of the right hand.
Be aware of this when bowing and put more pressure on these fingers when playing near the nut and less pressure when playing away from it. Doing so will help you to balance the bow and build up the muscles of your hand and forearm.
Do 15-20 bow strokes with this in mind before each practice session.

After familiarising oneself with the basic bowing technique, the next challenge is in crossing the strings while still maintaining a clean, distinct sound.

Exercises

When playing an E string followed by an A string the bow is required to move upwards and inwards. If this is continually repeated an anti-clockwise movement should result with the bow hand. Here are two exercises based on this theory:

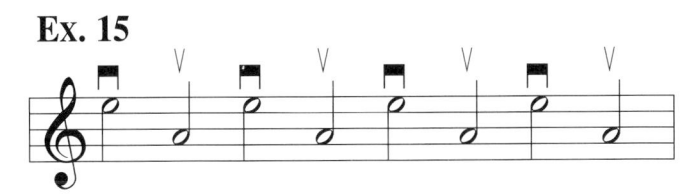

Ex. 15

BOW AND FOREARM MOVEMENT

The exact opposite results if the A string is bowed first:

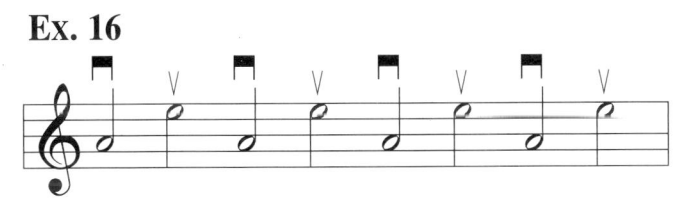

Ex. 16

Practise each version of the exercise very slowly at first, gradually speeding up as you become more familiar with it. Begin each exercise at roughly the centre of the bow, then begin closer to the nut where balancing the bow gets more difficult.

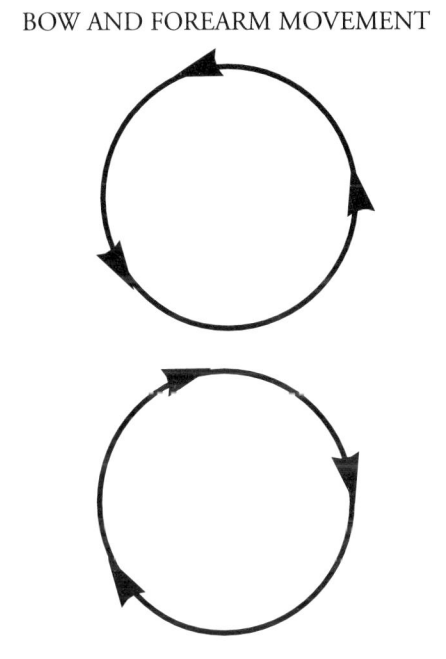

Attack on the bow is created by moving the bow at greater speed and by applying more pressure on the strings. Here are some bowing and rhythm exercises that will build up strength in the right arm, co-ordination and overall control of the bow:

(As the scale is one of the most basic bowing and fingering exercises, most of the bowing exercises are based on it.)

Here are a few exercise on open strings to begin with:

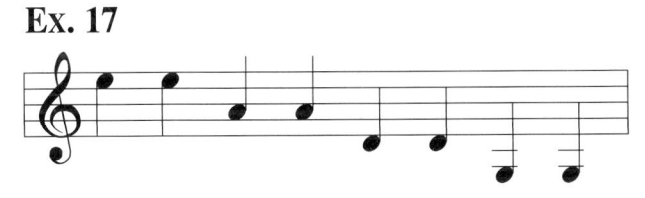

Ex. 17

Ex. 18

For each crotchet use roughly 1/2 the length of the bow.

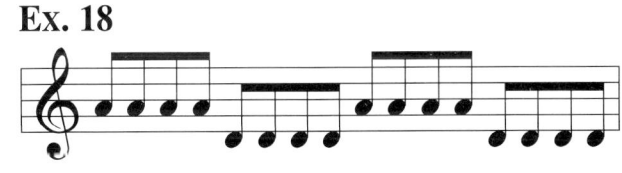

Use 1/4 of the bow for the quavers, and keep a firm grip on the bow.

Now try mixing crotchets and quavers:

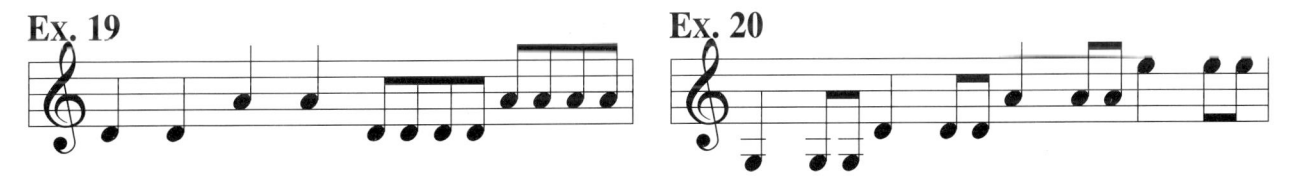

Ex. 19

Ex. 20

We'll work on rhythm now. Try counting these exercises before playing them.

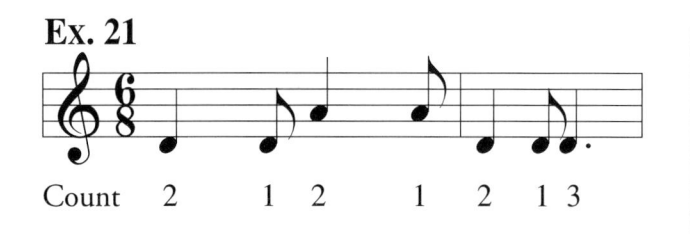

Ex. 21

Count   2   1   2   1   2   1   3

> Count 3 beats for a dotted crotchet
> 2 beats for a crotchet
> and 1 beat for a quaver

This is an example of some rhythms found often in jigs:

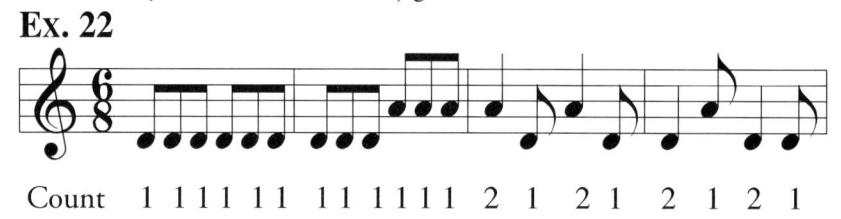

Ex. 22

Count   1 1 1 1 1 1   1 1 1 1 1 1   2   1   2   1   2   1   2   1

Next, we'll look at the slide rhythm, which has twice as many beats as a jig, thus having a time signature of 12/8.

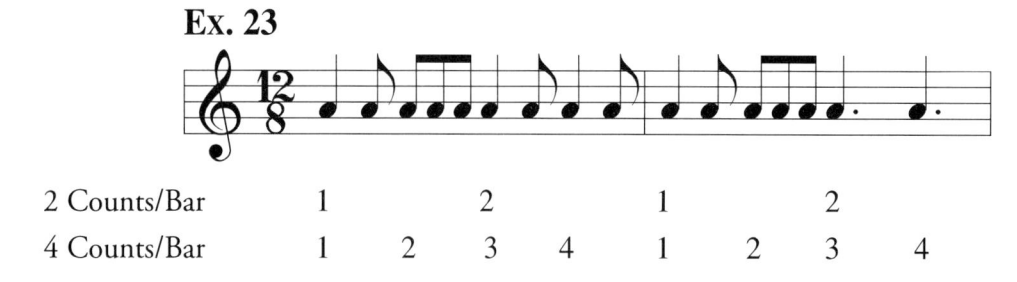

Ex. 23

2 Counts/Bar   1   2   1   2
4 Counts/Bar   1   2   3   4   1   2   3   4

Here are typical examples of rhythmic patterns in slides. The slide rhythm can be counted as 2 groups of 6 or 4 beats across the bar. As in the example above, dotted crotchets are also present in slides, often at the end of a part.

Here are just a couple more bowing exercises before we move on:

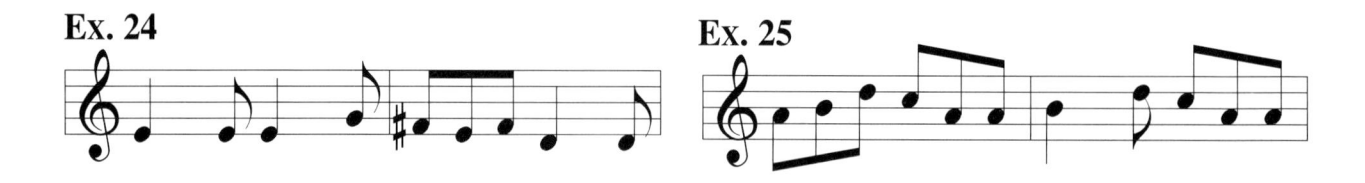

Ex. 24

Ex. 25

Remember: With all exercises, start on a down stroke and try to play them in reverse for additional practice.

Now we'll move on to more difficult exercises. These involve fingered notes and slurring across strings (see slurring section further on):

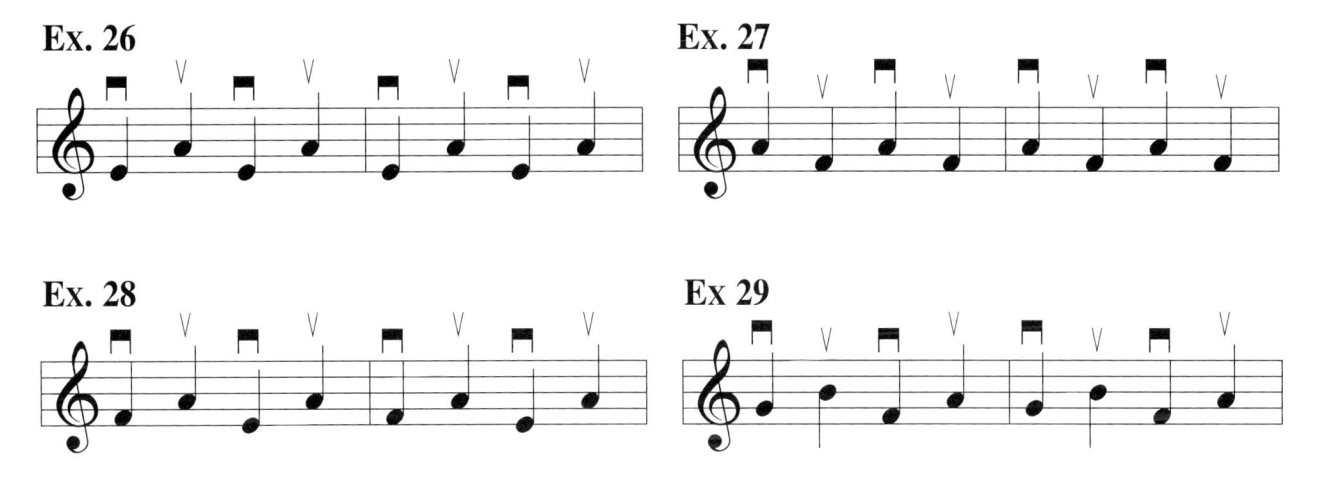

Ex. 26

Ex. 27

Ex. 28

Ex 29

Exaggerate the bowing for each exercise, and try to get a flowing movement of the bow.
You can try joining each one together (1 with 2, etc.), building up speed and consistency.

A useful exercise which is a slight variation on the circular bow movement is to slur (play more than one note in one stroke) across two strings back and forward, giving a similar forearm movement.

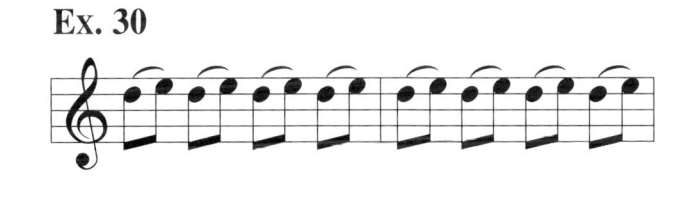

Ex. 30

BOW AND FOREARM MOVEMENT:

Put extra pressure on the bow as you cross the strings to hold definition of notes.

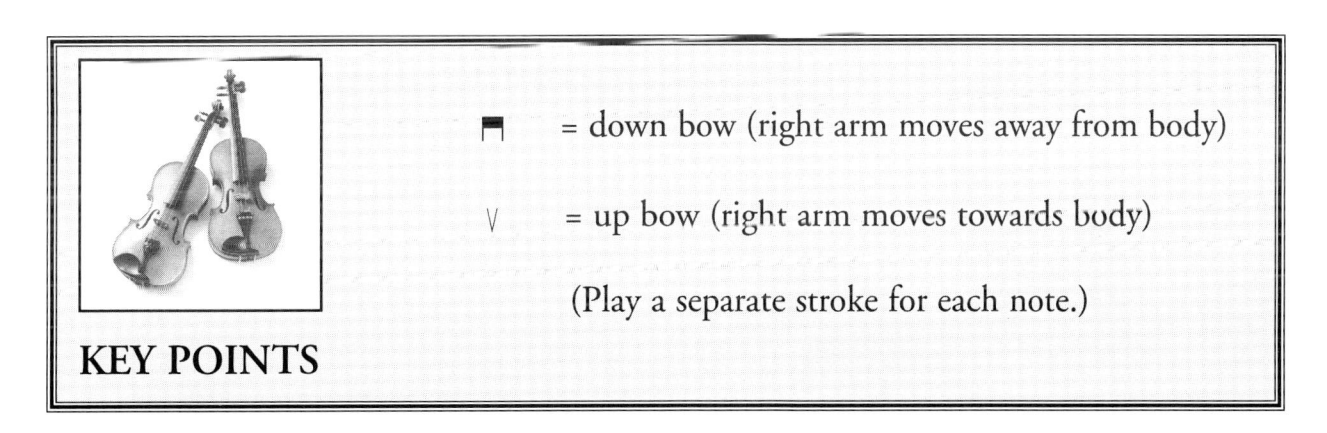

⊓ = down bow (right arm moves away from body)

V = up bow (right arm moves towards body)

(Play a separate stroke for each note.)

KEY POINTS

Slurring

Slurring means to play more than one note in the same bow stroke. When notes are slurred they sound smoother, creating a less rhythmic sound. Therefore, it is important to find a balance between slurring and playing separate bows. The more complex the bar structure, the more important it is to put proper thought as to where to slur.

Here are some slurring exercises using open strings only:

Ex. 31

Ex. 32

The next few exercises involve the use of fingered notes whilst slurring. Practise them very slowly at first until you feel comfortable, then try them at a faster pace.

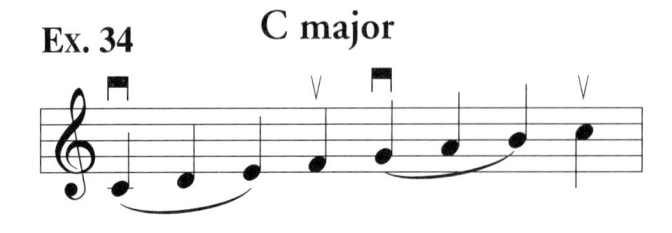

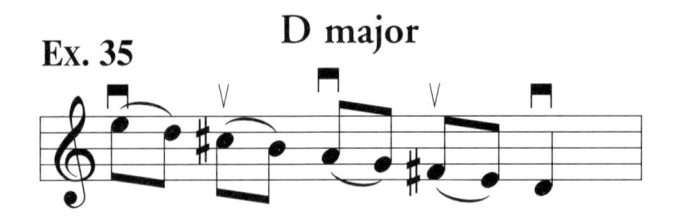

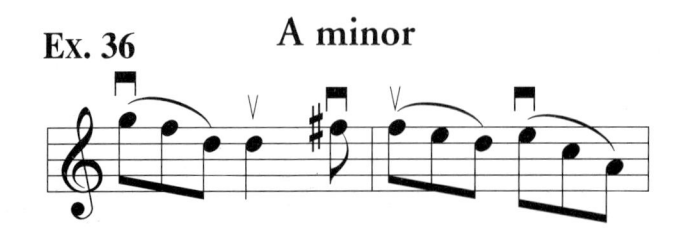

Ex. 33 D major

Ex. 34 C major

Ex. 35 D major

Ex. 36 A minor

Ex. 37 G major

Here is an example of slurring in the popular jig "The Lark in the Morning":

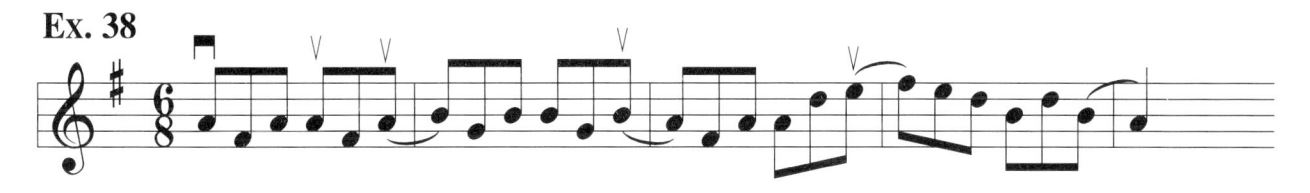

Ex. 38

KEY POINTS

Note: Keep the fingers of the left hand low and close to the fingerboard.

Some of the latter exercises may prove very difficult at first, but persevere and you will improve in bow control and technique.

When you place your thumb on the black tape, aim to play with the upper half of the bow in order to maintain the optimum balance. Most of the pressure on the bow comes from the first finger. This pressure should be lighter for slower tunes. In this way, the muscles of your hand will strengthen over time.

The bow should be played parallel to the bridge at all times.

The bow should be played close to the end of the fingerboard to give the softer sound preferred for traditional music

Style

Every player has his or her own style, reflecting their personal history, their technical ability and most of all, the things they are trying to express in their music. When you become proficient enough, you should decide on a particular style. Nobody's style is completely original. All players emulate certain other players to create an individual style, and the fiddle provides great flexibility with regard to the range of sounds that can be achieved. Elements of style can include tempo, ornamentation, and treatment of the melodic and rhythmic outline of the music. It is best for a beginner to learn a few pieces by a performer whose style one is particularly drawn to. A style of your own should eventually evolve.

There are many regional and local styles. As I have already mentioned, many styles have become eroded or mixed with others to form highly individualistic styles. Here are some of the broader regional styles, with equally broad definitions:

Donegal and the North

The music from this region tends to be played quite fast, with great energy and attack. Because of this, less time is spent on melodic variation and finger ornamentation and more on bowing. Droning is often used and piping ornamentation frequently imitated, such as cranning (a complex piping ornament that involves inserting extra notes into a melodic line). In general, bow strokes are kept short and can be highly syncopated.

There are many great exponents of the style, such as **James Byrne**, **Tommy Peoples** and **Vincent Campbell**. A pivotal figure in Donegal fiddling has been the late **Johnny Doherty**, one of the last of a class of travelling musicians and storytellers. There are a few recordings available by him (see discography). Tunes such as Highlands and Strathspeys are particular to the Northern region, with a strong influence from Scottish fiddling also.

Sligo

The Sligo style has been a dominant force in Irish fiddling this century. The music of Sligo featured heavily during the '20s, '30s and '40s. **James Morrison**, **Michael Coleman** and **Paddy Killoran** all emigrated to the U.S., bringing with them their regional styles. They all hailed from the same area, in and around Ballymote. The result of this cultural shift has produced some great protégés such as **Andy McGann** who was taught by **Michael Coleman** in New York for some time.

The style itself is usually up-tempo, with a nice mixture of rolling and trebling. Slurring of notes coupled with complex bowing gives Sligo playing a more rounded style than many others.

Galway and Clare

Many young players in Galway and Clare seem to possess the wisdom and experience of older players, a testament to the previous generation and the strength of the tradition in this region. The music of these counties has a characteristic sound, with an especially distinctive style of fiddle playing. Many variations of style occur locally.

Clare music, especially with older players, is perhaps the slowest of the many tempos in Irish music. As a result there is much melodic variation and a lot of complex and subtle ornamentation. In some areas an off-beat rhythm exists, adding to the music immensely.

Within the style itself, many notes are played on one bow stroke, with half to quarter tone sliding also present. The left hand adds much decorative ornamentation which complements the bow work very well. Of the many great players some do stand out. From previous generations, players such as **P.J. Hayes**, **Bobby Casey**, and **Junior Crehan** influenced and inspired many. Some of the young offspring of such a strong tradition would be **Tola Custy**, **Siobhán Peoples** and **Martin Hayes**. Clare is also represented in the States through players such as **Seamus Connolly** and **James Kelly**.

In Galway, one player has been prominent for many years. **Frankie Gavin** has been consistently gracing the airwaves since the early '70s and is a founder member of the group De Danann. Frankie's style is reminiscent of the driving swing associated with players of the 1920s. Other players strong in the Galway tradition would be **Paddy Fahey** and **Aggie White**. The style itself can be slow and expressive (e.g. Paddy Fahey) or fast and technically complex (e.g. Frankie Gavin).

Brendan McGlinchey and Joe Burke

Kerry and Cork

The area of Sliabh Luachra in the South West and on the border is home to a strong fiddling tradition. **Padraig O'Keeffe** (1887-1963) from Castleisland was a prominent performer and teacher. Other names also crop up, such as **Denis Murphy** (after whom many tunes are named) and his sister **Julia Clifford.**

The style of Kerry fiddle music is quite simple, with the melody often adhering to the original composition. Slides and polkas are the most popular type of tune, as set dancing has been popular in the region for many years. There is great drive in the music, with a rhythmic vitality hard to match anywhere else in the country.

Cork has a similar definition to that of Kerry. A man who has made a significant contribution over the years is **Seamus Creagh**. His duet with Kanturk accordionist **Jackie Daly** made a big impact in 1977. Another name of prominence in Cork is **Matt Cranitch,** who comes from a strong musical background and is an excellent reference for slow air playing.

Of course, there are many other regional styles, but discussions on styles would require much additional printed material and research. I hope this gives you a basic idea of the elements of style and the ideas needed to form your own.

Danny Magner, Castletownroche

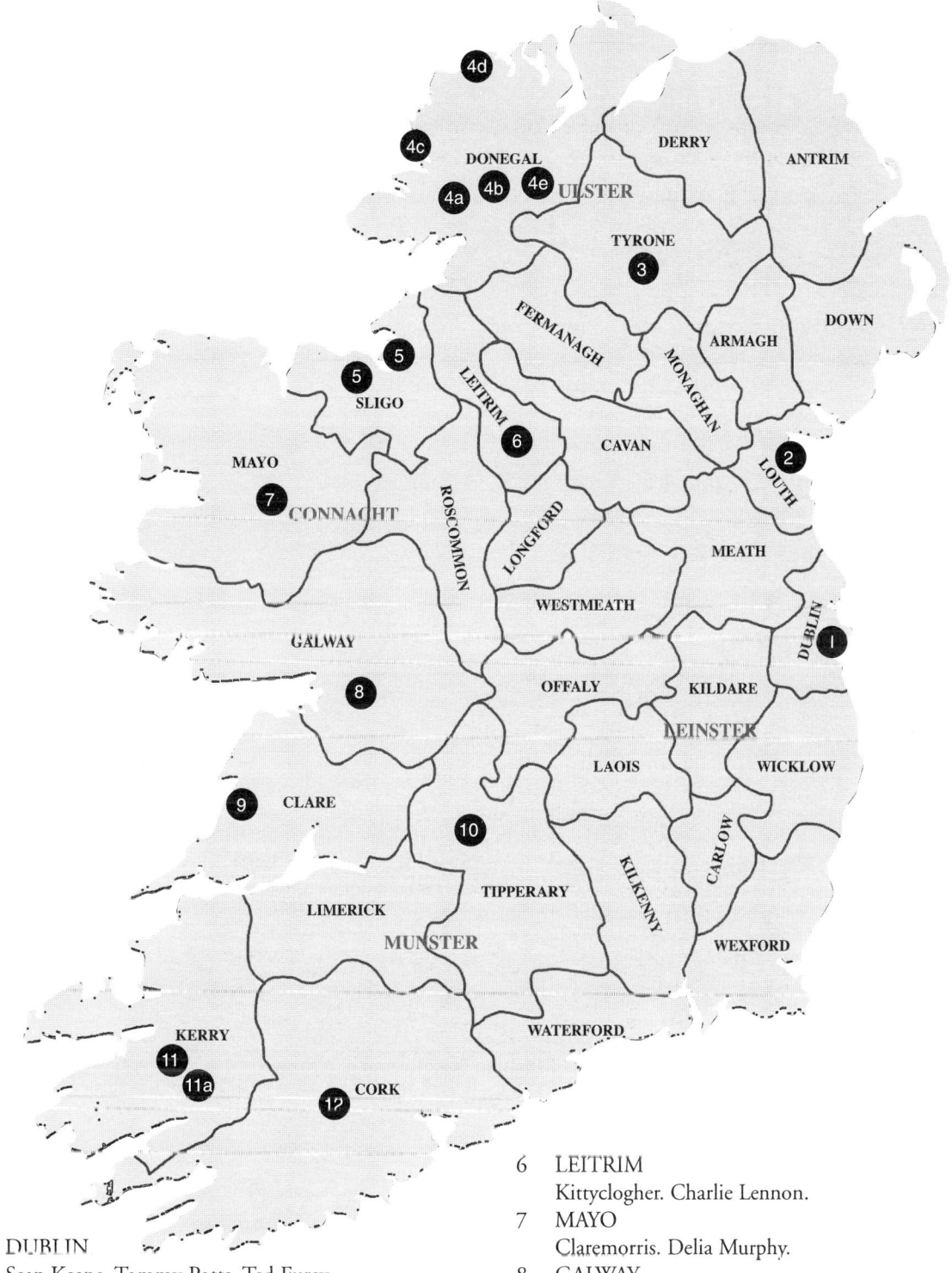

1. DUBLIN
   Sean Keane, Tommy Potts, Ted Furey.
2. LOUTH
   Dundalk. Gerry O'Connor
3. TYRONE
   Pomeroy. Cathal Hayden.
4. DONEGAL
   4a Glenties. Vincent Cambell.
   4b Ballybofey. Hughie Gillespie
   4c Dungloe. Neil O'Boyle.
   4d North West Donegal. Tom Glackin
   4e East Donegal. Tommy Peoples.
5. SLIGO
   James Morrison, Paddy Killoran, Micheal Coleman. Paddy Sweeney.
6. LEITRIM
   Kittyclogher. Charlie Lennon.
7. MAYO
   Claremorris. Delia Murphy.
8. GALWAY
   Corrandulla. Frankie Gavin.
9. CLARE.
   P.J Hayes, Bobby Casey, Vincent Griffin, Paddy Canny, John Kelly, Junior Crehan, Tony Linnane.
10. TIPPERARY
    Nenagh. Sean Ryan
11. KERRY
    Castleisland. Padraig O'Keefe.
    11a Cork/Kerry (Sliabh Luachra) Denis Murphy, Julia Clifford, Paddy Cronin.
12. CORK
    Seamus Creagh

35

Ornamentation (1)

Ornamentation is the primary form of expression outside the musical piece. It should decorate the tune without upsetting the melody. Here is the first and most basic of all finger ornamentation, the cut:

The Cut

The cut (also known as the single grace note) is used very effectively to separate two notes of the same pitch; **both notes are applied in one bow stroke.** A cut is indicated by a crossed off note written smaller on the musical tablature.

To play a grace note, the finger stops the string momentarily by lightly pressing the string. Note that the string is not required to touch the fingerboard, because the stopped note is not actually heard. Only the breaking of two notes is required. Here are a couple of examples:

Ex. 39

Ex. 40

KEY POINTS

A quick flick of the finger is needed to play a cut.

The bow must be moving smoothly and quickly to bring out clarity and volume, although pressure on the bow is light.

Bring your finger slightly across the string as you flick. Cuts are easier to perform at speed this way; watch other players doing this.

It is commonplace to bring your fingers away from the fingerboard just before playing the cut. This is to build up power and speed (all-important when playing the cut). The fingers should then return to close above the fingerboard.

Different fingers are used for different cuts.

for cutting on an open string, use 2nd or 3rd finger.
for cutting a first finger note, use 2nd or 3rd finger.
for cutting a 2nd finger note, use the 3rd finger.
for cutting a 3rd finger position, use the 4th finger.

Note: When cutting the third finger note, the fourth does not have to play the next note up; just the stopping of the string is required. Anywhere above the third finger will do.

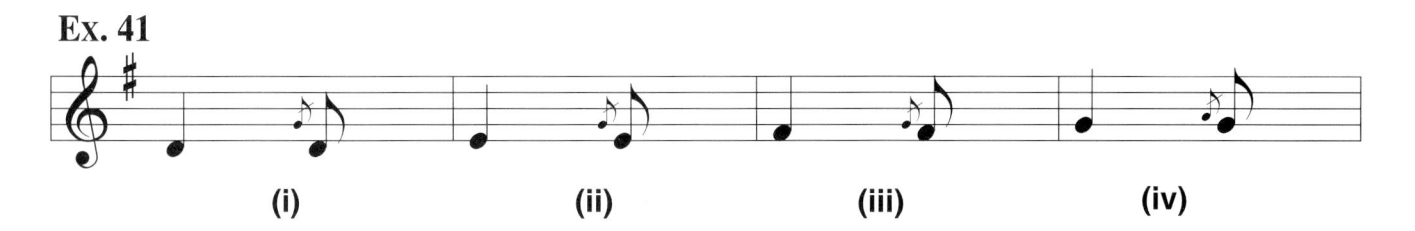

Cut Practice

Ex. 41

(i) (ii) (iii) (iv)

Note:
The grace note is played without upsetting the rhythm in the time signature.

When playing the above, remember one stroke for each example. If (iv) proves difficult it is because of the generally weak fourth finger. Strength will build up over time.

The Double Cut

The double cut is similar to the cut. Two grace notes one of which is also the main note, are involved. It is written as in the example below:

Ex. 42

The first of these grace notes is played a split second before the finger flicks to produce the upper grace note. The double cut, unlike the cut, does not separate two notes of the same pitch, but adds attack and rhythm to the main note. Because grace notes do not affect the rhythm, much listening and practice is needed to bring the double cut up to the required speed.

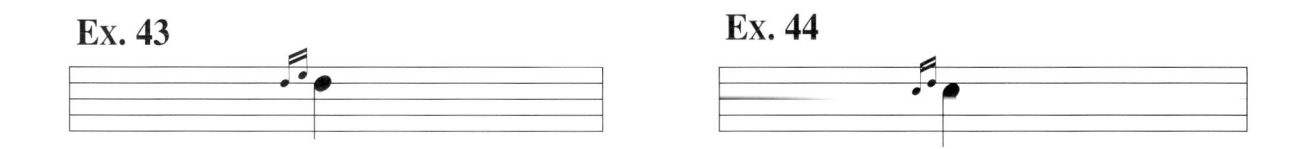

Ex. 43

The D is played just before flicking the fourth finger to produce a double cut on D.

Ex. 44

The C is played just before flicking the third finger to produce a double cut on C.

The double cut is fingered ornamentation and is played in one bow stroke.

Triplets

A triplet is an ornament that uses the bow to play three notes of equal timing in the space of two notes — for instance, three quavers played in the time of 2 quavers (1 crotchet). In faster tunes such as reels, the triplet is often the same note, e.g.

Ex. 45

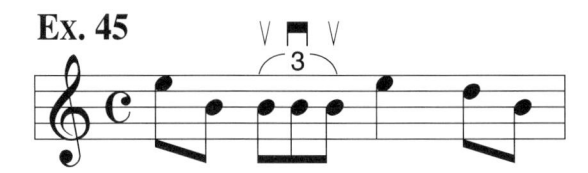

Above, a common reel triplet. (A triplet can have a quaver before it, often being the same note as in the example above.) Triplets, especially those using the same note, are often referred to as **trebling** (see advanced ornamentation).

Ex. 46

A triplet in the "Boys of Blue Hill" hornpipe. Triplets are often played on open strings for the extra tone and because rolls (see page 40.) in the strict sense are not possible.

Triplets occur in various forms, some borrowed from reed and wind instruments.
Here are some examples:

Ex. 47

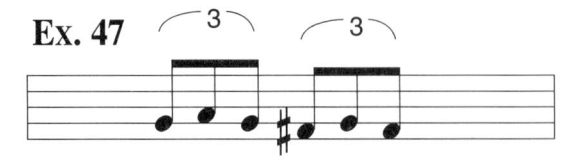

A triplet involving two strings. The fourth finger can be added to play A on the D string.

Ex. 48

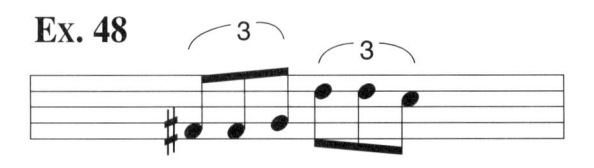

In these triplets, the first two notes of the triplet are the same. The finger and bow coordination can be awkward, so spend more time practising this one.

Ex. 49

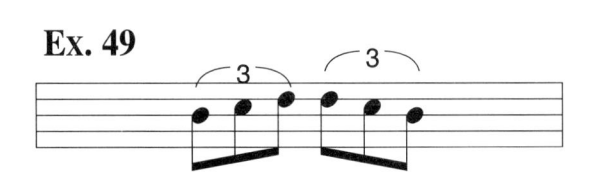

The most basic of all triplets, ascending or descending.

Ex. 50

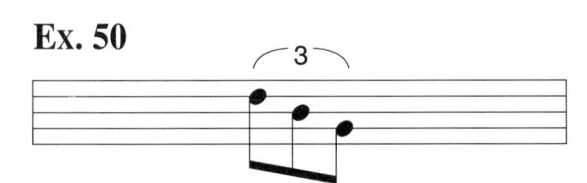

A triplet with a gap of two notes between each note of the triplet. Used for slower pieces, especially set dances.

KEY POINTS — It is easier to control the bow when playing triplets around the upper half of the bow, so start practising there first.

> Remember to keep the bow strokes extremely short for triplets.
>
> Playing a triplet is just a flick of the wrist, not a movement of the whole arm. The arm and forearm should be tightened and the wrist loose in order to do the flick required.
>
> Practise triplets starting in both directions.

KEY POINTS

Placement of Triplets

This will take much playing experience, but here are some ideas for inserting them:

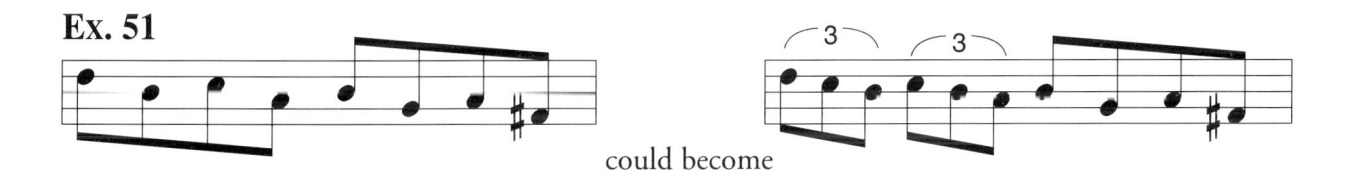

Ex. 51

could become

A triplet can also fall on a crotchet:

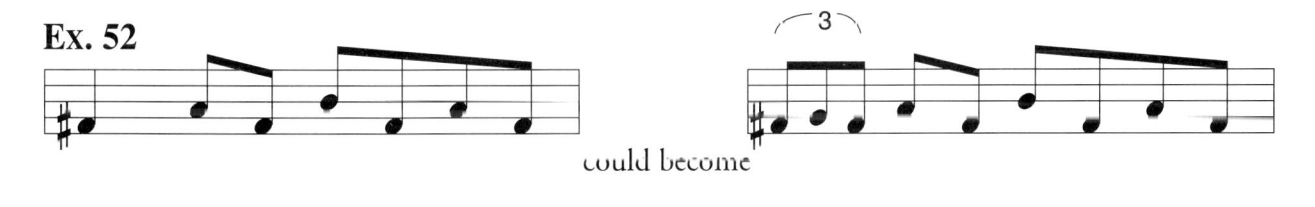

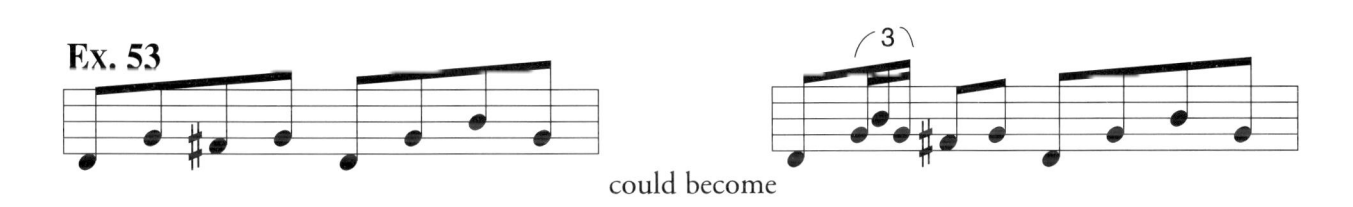

Ex. 52

could become

Ex. 53

could become

The bowing of triplets is very much left up to the player. In hornpipes, many are generally played in separate bows to add to the rhythm, whereas in reels they are mostly slurred.

The Roll

The roll is the most important form of ornamentation in Irish music. There are basically two types of roll, the long roll and the short roll. When playing a roll, the emphasis is placed on the main note.

Long Rolls

The long roll consists of five notes played in the time of a dotted crotchet. Long rolls are more common in jigs. Here's how a long roll on G would look:

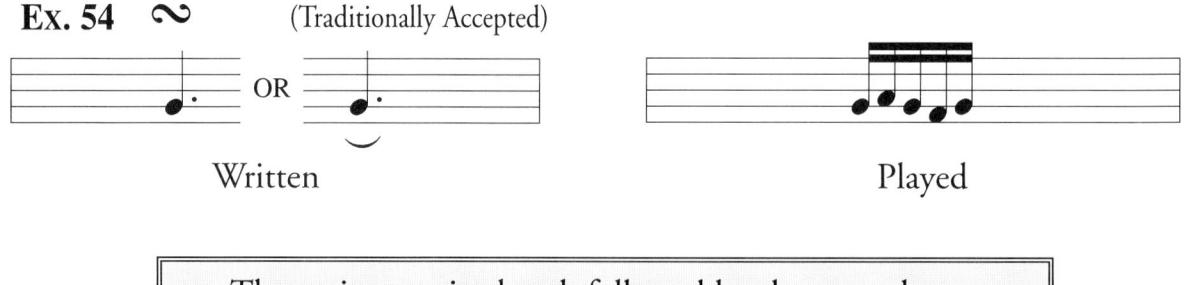

Ex. 54   (Traditionally Accepted)

Written   Played

> The main note is played, followed by the note above,
> the main note again, the note below and
> once more the main note.

The roll can be written in different ways. A G roll could also look like

OR

How to Play Rolls

All five notes of a roll are played in one bow stroke. Think of the roll as having three beats.

Ex. 55

1   2   3   Played   Written

Three F notes with three pulses   An F roll containing three less obvious pulses

The first finger roll differs slightly from the others in that the second or third finger can be used for the higher note of the roll. The roll is played so quickly that the difference is not noticeable.

We have already covered F (2nd finger) and G (3rd finger) rolls; a first finger roll would look like this:

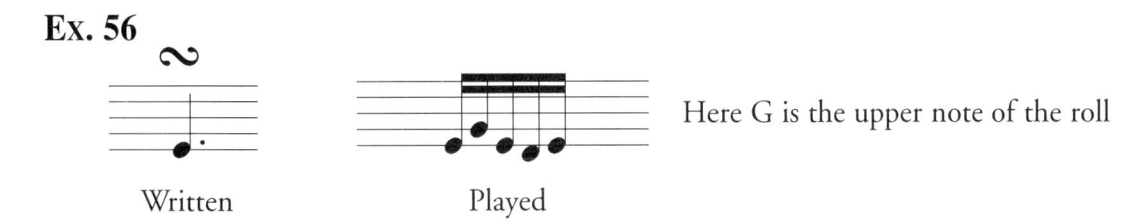

Ex. 56

Written   Played   Here G is the upper note of the roll

The purpose of the upper note is to achieve the rhythmic character of the roll as when cutting. Therefore this note is inconsequential, eg., when playing an E roll (D string) cut with the 2nd or 3rd finger then quickly lift off the first finger to finish.

A roll on an open string is not practical because you would need to cross strings to play the lower note of the roll. Therefore, a variation of the roll is played with two auxiliary notes above the main note:

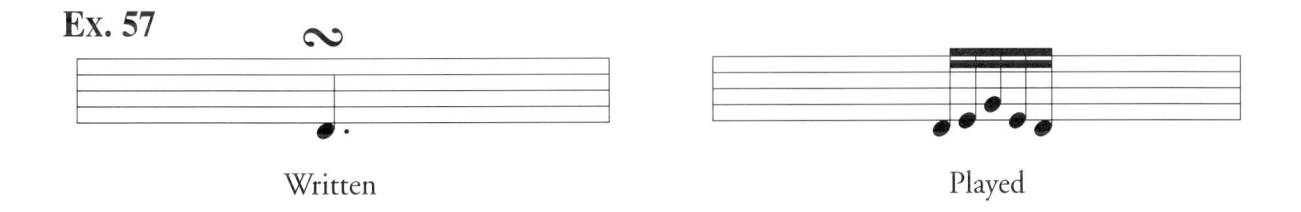

Ex. 57

Written   Played

The G note here is played with a quick flick of the third finger. (Because this is technically difficult to master, many fiddlers would put other ornamentation here such as a triplet, melodic variation, etc.) Long rolls mostly have a quaver after them taking up half a bar. Remember that long rolls are always dotted crotchets.

Here are a couple of examples:

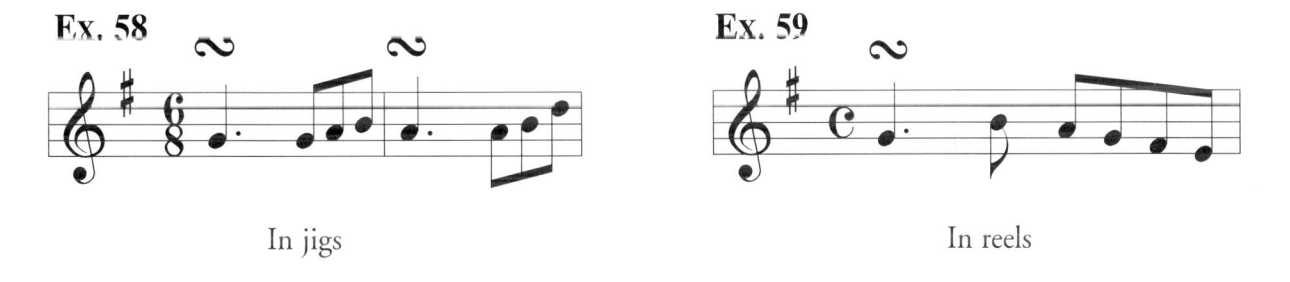

Ex. 58   **Ex. 59**

In jigs   In reels

Short Rolls

Like the long roll, the short roll contains five notes and is completed in one bow stroke. The short roll is played within the time of a crotchet only, hence the name.

Broken down one could look like

Ex. 60

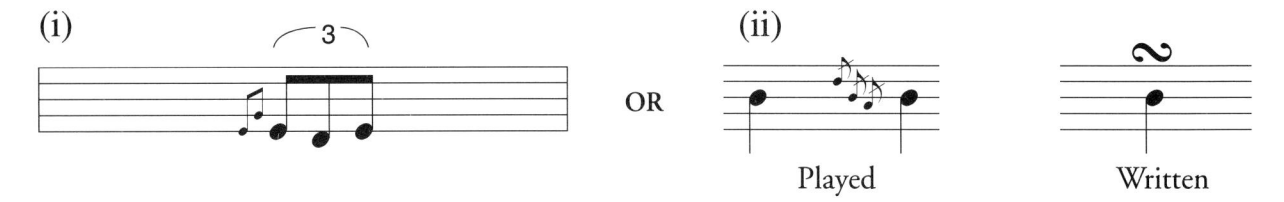

(i)   OR   (ii)

                                                        Played   Written

The short roll can be best understood as a triplet preceded by two grace notes, with the first note of the triplet being rolled. Because of the speed at which short rolls are played, they can be altered slightly, giving the same effect.

Example (i) could also be

Here four notes are used for the crotchet roll. This example would be more suited to the button accordion, as five notes played in such a short space of time require much strength and dexterity. With most beginners short rolls will take at least a couple of months to play properly, so persevere.

KEY POINTS

Lean a little heavier on the bow when playing short rolls to emphasise rhythm and attack.

The relative lengths of notes in a roll can vary from one player to the next, so listen to the cassette and to other styles of playing.

Here are some examples of short rolls:

In Reels

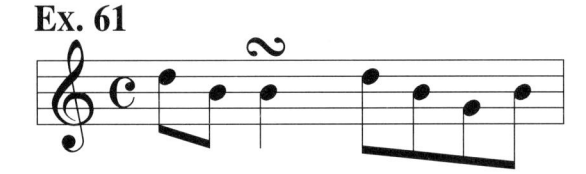

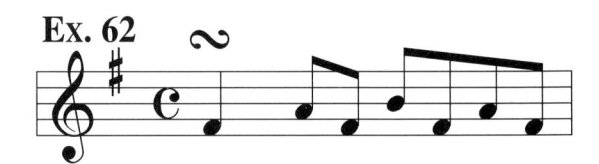

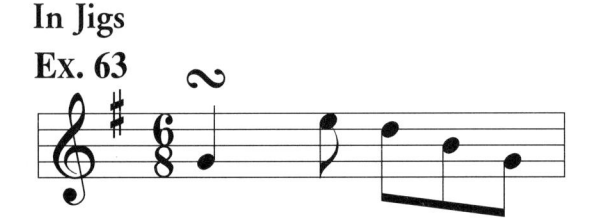

Ex. 61   **Ex. 62**

In Jigs

Ex. 63   **Ex. 64**

Tied Rolls

To play the full five notes of a roll on a crotchet at speed would prove difficult even to the experienced player. A variation of the roll can be played only if the roll is preceded by the same note.

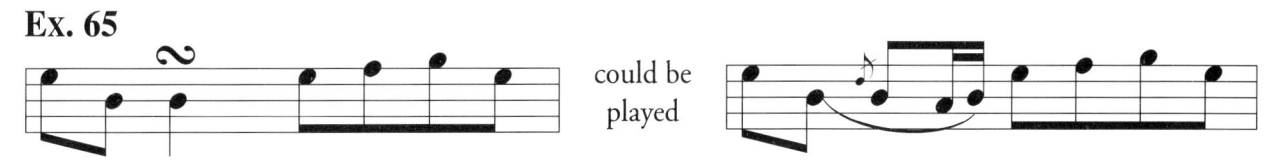

Ex. 65   could be played

Tied rolls make the task of playing a roll easier while sounding very similar to the written music. Here are two more examples:

Ex. 66   could be played

Ex. 67   could be played

As with the roll itself, the variation is played in one stroke.

REVIEW

(1) With the basics now covered, review them again, concentrating on posture and hold of the instrument. It is very important at this stage to avoid bad habits.

(2) Learn by heart the notes and their positions on the fingerboard. Learn one string first and use that as a reference in finding the other notes.

(3) Don't get bogged down with music theory; it's only there to help you to read the music.

(4) I would recommend practising for about 20-30 minutes at least three times a week in order to make real progress. Have a goal when practising, to achieve over the session.

(5) Be relaxed and quite loose when playing; there are no hard and fast rules on how to hold the fiddle in traditional music. Keep adjusting until you are comfortable – this will stand to you later when you need to play faster. When you are comfortable with the hold, stick to it!

(6) Now we'll move on. The next few sections include more session-worthy tunes such as jigs, slip jigs and hornpipes.

Jigs

When musicians refer to jigs they often mean double jigs (where the time signature is 6/8). There are two other types of jig: The slip jig (9/8) and the single jig (12/8), both of which we will discuss later.

The look of a jig is more predictable than that of other types of tunes. A bar often has six notes with ornamentation, or crotchet pauses, occasionally changing that to four or seven. The last bar of each part often contains four notes, the last note mostly being a dotted crotchet.

Here is an old song in jig timing called 'Johnny I Hardly Knew Ye':

Ex. 68

While going the road to sweet A-thy a roo — ha roo — while going the road to sweet A-thy a roo —

Most jig tunes have more notes in each bar and would be played fast, but this should give you a good idea. Have a look at this first jig to see some more typical jig bars.

Máirséail Francach
(MAGUIRE'S MARCH)

Although the tune has 6/8 time signature, it is played much slower – more like a march.

Ex. 69

Jig

Out In The Ocean

This tune has always been a favourite of mine since I heard the great '70s band Planxty record a particularly nice version. In recent years it has become popular to play the tune in the key of A.

Ex. 70   Jig

The Old Favourite

This is a lovely old Clare jig with a nice lilt to it. When the tune becomes more familiar to you, substitute B rolls in bars 1 and 5 and high G rolls in bars 17 and 21.

Ex. 71 *Jig*

Garret Barry's Jig

This jig in G is a popular jig with uilleann pipers. Some possible variations are given below.

Ex. 72

Ex. 73 Here are two variations of bar 1:

Ex. 74 The last bar of the first part could be

This produces a cranning effect similar to uilleann piping.

It is the norm to vary ornamentation each time you play a part. In the second part you can put in a run, so bar 10 would be

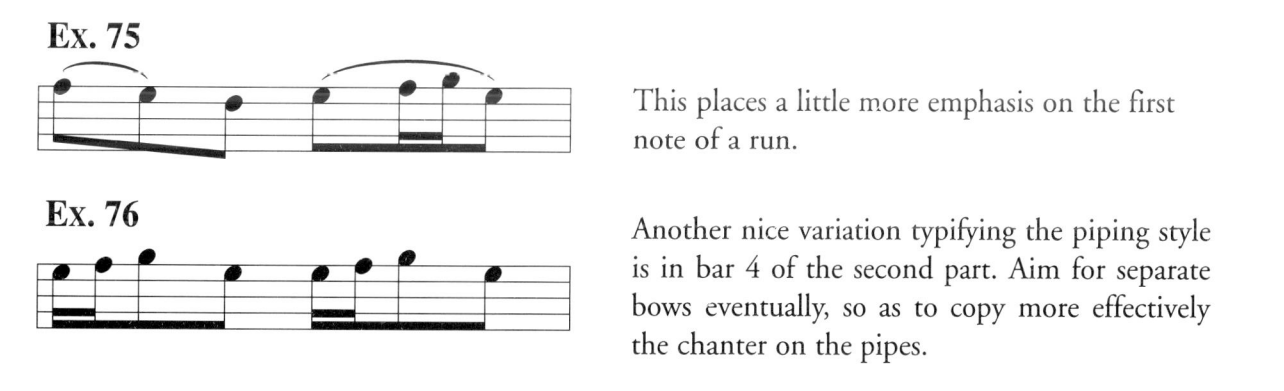

Ex. 75

This places a little more emphasis on the first note of a run.

Ex. 76

Another nice variation typifying the piping style is in bar 4 of the second part. Aim for separate bows eventually, so as to copy more effectively the chanter on the pipes.

Morrrison's Jig

Ex. 77

Double Stop (Ending Chord E minor)

Jig

For any of the E or B rolls you can substitute the following if you find rolls difficult:

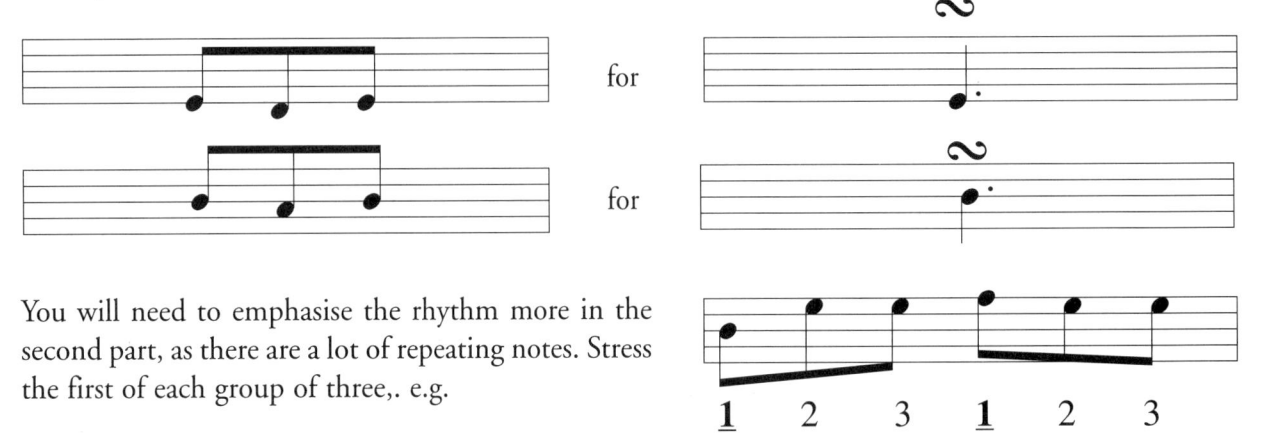

for

for

You will need to emphasise the rhythm more in the second part, as there are a lot of repeating notes. Stress the first of each group of three,. e.g.

1 2 3 1 2 3

Bow strokes should also be slightly shorter for beats 2 & 3.

The Hag's Purse

Ex. 78   Jig

Tunes in some keys will have naturals, and a scale playing naturals is good practice. Try this D scale, playing naturals for F and C. (This scale is called the Dorian Minor).

Ex. 79

You may need to lift the second finger off the string in order to comfortably play the third. This is allowed. Be careful not to adjust the hand position when playing this scale. Try also a low G and A scale with naturals.

The second part of the tune has an F natural (a semitone lower than F#) which is played closer to the nut than F#. For practice of this F you can practise the F major scale:

Ex. 80

The first F is played with the second finger close to the first; the high F is played very close to the nut. When trying this scale, listen closely to see if you are in tune. Notice the B♭, which is also close to the nut.

The Cliffs Of Moher

Ex. 81   Jig

A high A roll can be substituted for the first three notes in bar 1.

Ornamentation (2)

Here are some further examples of ornamentation in Jigs and Reels.

Coppers and Brass (3rd Part)

Ex. 82

Could become

In this popular piping tune, notes can be doubled to form triplets and add extra bite to the rhythm.

A similar effect can be employed at the beginning of the 'Cliffs of Moher'

Ex. 83

This type of ornament can also occur in reels, eg. 'Music in the Glen'

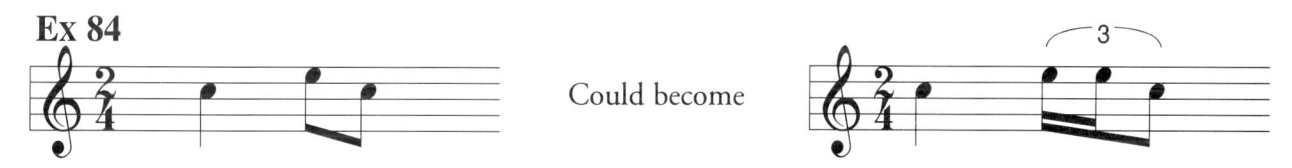

Ex 84

Could become

The 'Steampacket' reel could also have an alternate first bar.

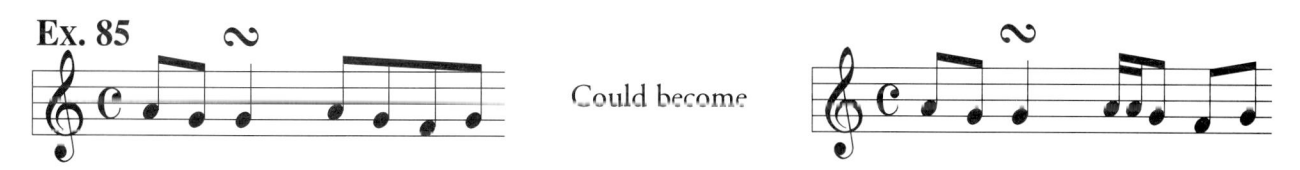

Ex. 85

Could become

Short Roll Ornamentation in Jigs

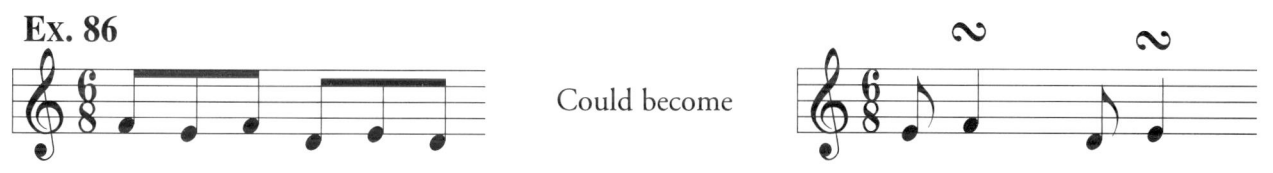

Ex. 86

Could become

Here above is a variation of the third bar of 'Banish Misfortune', again this closely mimics a piping style.

Try inserting these variations into some of the tunes at the back of the book. However, I would advise you to listen to other players playing them first before trying them yourself.

Slip Jigs

Slip jigs are a much neglected type of tune most often heard at dancing Feiseanna, where they are regarded as a type of dance. The time signature is 9/8, with nine pulses per bar, best counted as three groups of three.

I have used a popular nineteenth century ballad to explain the slip jig rhythm in the form of 'The Rocky Road to Dublin':

Ex. 87

In the mer - ry month of May . . .

Most slip jigs have a light, airy sound which suits the fiddle well. Slip jigs sound just as nice slowed down and are therefore good tunes on which to practise rolls (see ornamentation).

The Butterfly

Ex. 88   Slip Jig

In the second bar of line 2 (the second part) your 2nd finger should cover the A and E strings. This makes going from C natural to G natural much easier.

Coleman's Slip Jig

Ex. 89 Slip Jig

Thug Mé Rúide

The triplet in each part should be played with separate bows, and it has two beats.

Ex. 90 Slip Jig

The Blackhaired Lass

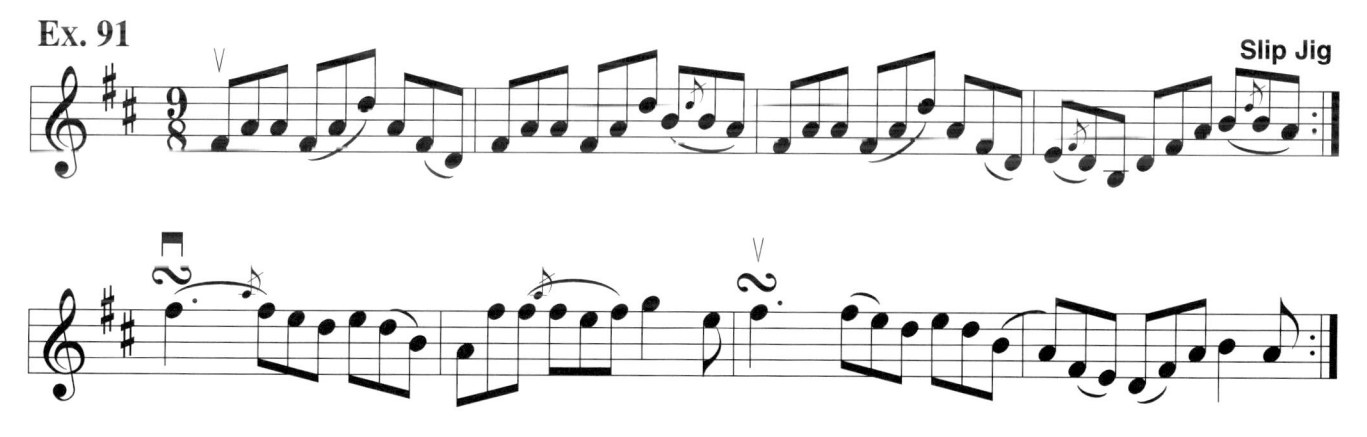

Ex. 91 Slip Jig

Tommy Peoples

The Instruments - Continued

The violin was introduced from Italy around the mid 16th century and what we know today as the native Irish or Union pipes developed nearly a century later. As an instrument easily adapted to dance tunes, the fiddle vied with the pipes for popularity and was enjoying a healthy place in cultural esteem by the end of the 17th century. The fiddle was perhaps cheaper and more easily come by than the pipes, but more importantly, the fingering was flexible and allowed the accommodation of all forms of ornamentation. Though the pipes had a dominating influence on popular dance music, the body of dance music played today was undoubtedly written by fiddlers, such as the great wealth of slow reels or strathspeys which originated in Scotland. By the mid 18th century the fiddle was outpacing the pipes in popularity, and though the pipes are enjoying a renewed status today, they were in such decline in the early 1900's that the disgruntled piper John Smithwick from Cork was moved to pen the verse found on Page 4.

Continued on P.58

Hornpipes

Hornpipes have for years been a showcase for talent and technical ability on the fiddle. In recent years, their playing has mostly been reserved for solo and céilí dancing.

The time signature of a hornpipe is in fact the same as a reel, 4/4 or C. It is usual to count two beats per bar, as in a reel. In notating the hornpipe, the second note of each bar is a semiquaver and the first is a dotted crotchet. Playing a hornpipe exactly as written results in the tune being rigid, losing any flow the piece might contain. Therefore, the rhythm of hornpipes is not quite as strict. A couple of listens to the tape will give you a good idea.

Here are a couple of bar examples:

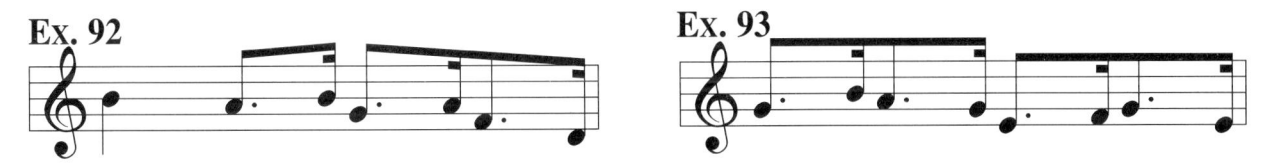

Ex. 92

Ex. 93

As you can see, there are two groups of four pulses with two counts. Vocally, the rhythm would come out as something like long short long short, etc.

The Plains Of Boyle

This is one of the older hornpipes and is often fancied for dance accompaniment

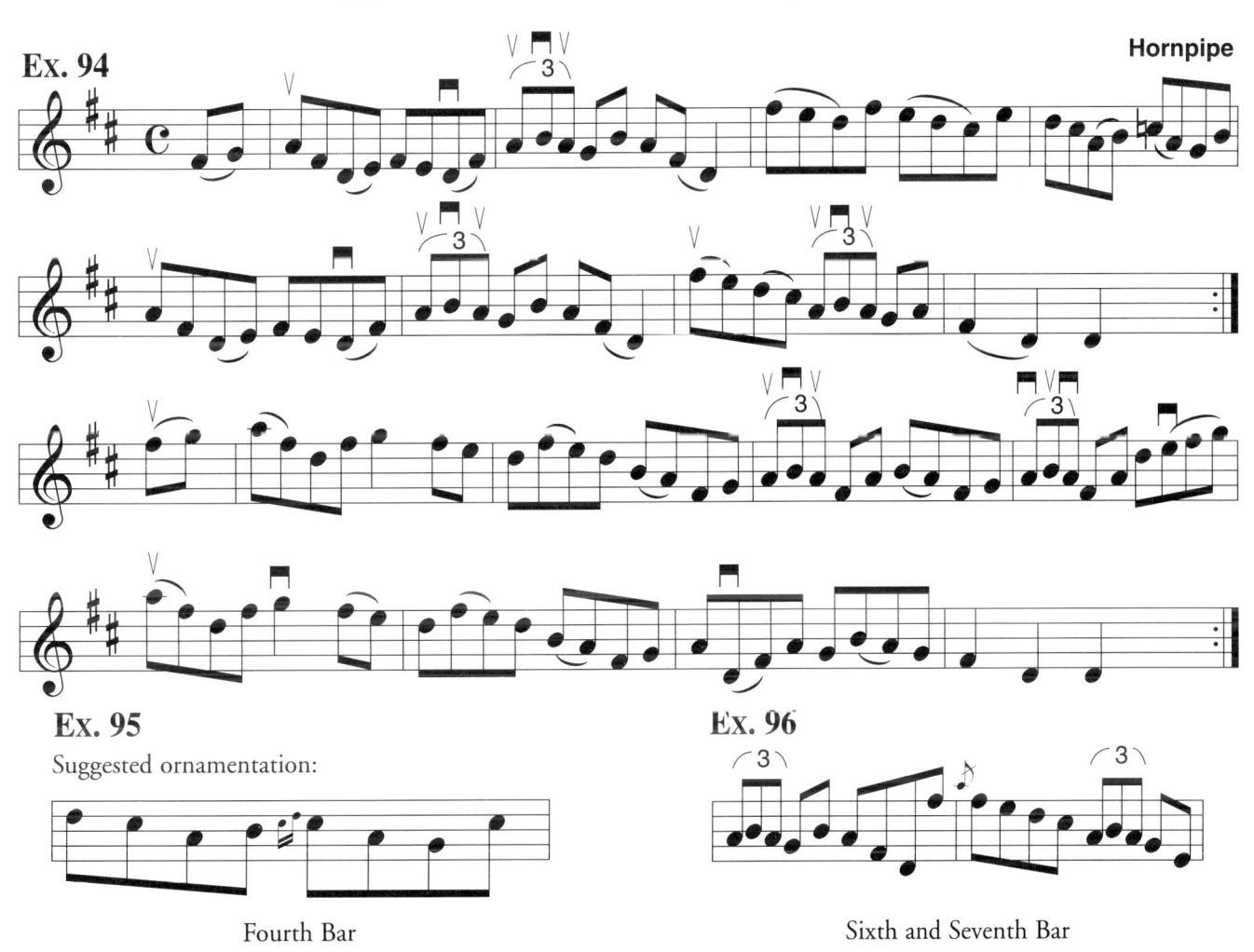

Ex. 94   Hornpipe

Ex. 95
Suggested ornamentation:

Fourth Bar

Ex. 96

Sixth and Seventh Bar

The Boys Of Blue Hill

This popular hornpipe should help you to understand rhythm and help you develop your bowing. Play it slowly and deliberately at first. As always, learn the notes before trying the marked bowing.

Ex. 97

Off To California

I first heard this hornpipe from the playing of the great Andy McGann, an Irish-American fiddler living in New York. Andy's playing is very sweet, his bowing very precise and his ornamentation subtle. Hardly surprising, for once Andy had a string of lessons from Michael Coleman when Michael would visit the McGann household.

Ex. 98

Alexander's Hornpipe

This is a lovely hornpipe with an arpeggio-like figure in the second part which will be good practice. When you see a grace note with a hook attached, it means to play the note immediately before the next, like a cut, rather than separating the two notes evenly. In this case, play the E with the fourth finger on the A string. Play the triplets with separate bows to bring out the rhythm.

Ex. 99 *Hornpipe*

Harvest Home

This has been a popular fiddle tune for many years in Ireland and Britain. It almost continuously bounces from string to string and is great practice for bowing. Slur the descending triplets in each part for now, working to play separate bows eventually. This will add to the to-ing and fro-ing as heard in the rest of the tune.

Ex. 100 *Hornpipe*

(clockwise wrist movement)

(anti-clockwise wrist movement)

KEY POINTS

You will no doubt find the difference in tempo difficult, so listen to the accompanying cassette, which covers some of the tunes in this section. Tap along, hum or even lilt the tunes to test yourself.

If you prefer you can leave the bowing instructions until you have an idea of the melody of the tune. You can still bow notes individually.

To understand and appreciate different styles of playing you will need to listen to players of different backgrounds and from various parts of the country (see map page). I would recommend anything by Johnny Doherty, the Donegal fiddler who has an exciting and vibrant approach to the music. If you have an opportunity to hear the music first hand by all means do so. Listen to recordings of fiddling in duets, trios, céilí bands, etc. It will give you an idea of how a player can adapt to play with other instruments. A comprehensive discography listing is at the back of the book.

Garret Barry's, Morrison's and the Cliffs of Moher are three jigs I would play regularly together in a session. Grouping tunes together in this way helps you to remember tunes and concentrate on perfecting them, making it easier to express your ideas.

Playing a set dance will take extra practice (as they are normally only played for dances and not as session tunes). If possible, watch solo step dancers to get the rhythm and feel of the set dance.

Throughout the book you will notice that many tunes may appear to be unresolved or have the incorrect amount of beats in the final bar. This is because most of the tunes are played in sets of 2 or 3, allowing a couple of beats to introduce the next tune, with the lead-in notes played each time round of the first tune.

The Instruments – Continued

In any event, the fiddle, harp and pipes are not at war today and are frequently found in sweet harmony amongst contemporary players. Unlike the Union pipes, the fiddle has no distinctively Irish characteristics to its make-up but it has developed styles of playing uniquely suited to Irish music, especially dance music. To an extent, the instrument used for composing will dictate elements of the structure of the tune, and the notes on which ornamentations occur may indicate the origin of the tune.

Style of fiddle playing is a combination of tradition, selection and improvisation. The fiddle is a common instrument in folk music the world around and is capable of many types of tonal variation. In the Irish tradition, however, the fiddler does not seek the sharp qualities of the classical player, but rather aims for a softer tone by bowing the instrument closer to the fingerboard.

However, there is no absolute standard, and regional variations are endless. Additionally, since the Irish style of fiddling is played in the first position there is no need to hold the instrument tucked firmly under the chin as classical players do. As long as there is no limit to the mobility of the fingers finding the notes, a variety of holds are available to the traditional player, ranging from chin to waist.

Continued on P.64

Set Dances

Set dances are not session tunes as such, but basic tunes which correspond to a set sequence of steps. They require subtle phrasing and distinct rhythm to be played properly for dancing. Good control of the bow is needed.

The rhythm of a set dance is generally 4/4, but some are played in 6/8 timing, that of a jig. A set dance is often written in the same way as a hornpipe in a dotted crotchet, semiquaver format. The rhythm is adhered to much more than a hornpipe, giving a strong rhythmical feel to the tune.

Structurally, set dances differ from other tunes. The first part has eight bars, but the second can have eight, twelve, fourteen or even sixteen bars.

The Roving Pedlar

Keep the pace very slow for set dances in general. The triplets in the second part will need some separate practice.

The Orange Rogue

This is one of the more popular set dances. You will need to give it a good listening, or even watch dancers perform it, to get the feel of the tune.

Ex. 102   **Set Dance**

THE SLOW AIR derives from old Gaelic songs often sung in the sean-nós style (old style). Some slow airs correspond to ballads, others are purely instrumental pieces. There is also another type of air: Those composed by Turlough Ó Carolan (b.1670, Co. Meath). He became blind through illness at the age of eighteen and set out on his life as an itinerant harper, travelling around Ireland for nearly fifty years. He entertained patrons in their own houses, often composing pieces in their honour! Unlike sean-nós style airs, O'Carolan's music has a fixed musical metre. The slow air can include many types of ornamentation and have a dreamier and more expressive feel than many other Irish pieces. Ornamentation should link and decorate musical phrases (originally vocal phrases) and should be natural and unobtrusive to the melody. Fewer and fewer people are learning airs directly from sean-nós singing. This is because the Irish language is confined to the Gaeltacht areas in certain parts of the country. Listening to recordings of sean-nós singers would help enormously in the understanding and full appreciation of the art of good slow air playing.

Port na bPúcaí

Ex. 103   Slow Air

Planxty Irwin

Ex. 104

O'Carolan

Bunclody

Ex. 105

Slow Air

Polkas And Slides

Polkas and Slides are more directly associated with dancing than any other type of Irish tune. Sliabh Luachra (see Style Article P.32) has produced some pivotal figures in the development of traditional music this century. Denis Murphy, Julia Clifford (brother and sister) and Pádraig O Keefe were all great exponents from this region.

The polka has a very simple rhythm. It has a time signature of 2/4 and is perhaps the easiest to understand of traditional tunes. There are two beats in each bar often comprising of a simple four quaver pattern. If you have any problems with the rhythm in the following polkas refer to the 'Kerry Polka' at the beginning of the book (P.23).

The Slide or single jig has a time signature of 12/8 and has its origins in the dance of the same name. Like the polka, the slide has great lift and swing. Much of the rhythm is created from the bow-hand in preference to using left hand ornamentation. To compensate for the lack of fingered ornamentation various embellishments have evolved such as double stopping and droning (see advanced ornamentation)

Johnny Leary's Polka

In this first polka I would recommend that you slur the semiquavers in bars 2 and 6. Watch out for the G# accidental in the second part.

Ex. 106

Duggan's Polka

Ex. 107   Polka

IRISH MUSIC
The Styles of Playing

Today, very little traditional music can be classed as purely instrumental, that is, intended for pure listening rather than marching or dancing. Considering the magical attributes so often ascribed to the harp in mythology, it may be safe to deduce that in earlier times such was not the case. However, it is likely that the tunes played today are of greater antiquity than the songs, since shifts in language and culture more quickly wipe out a song tradition that incorporate it. Tunes, however, adapt easily as do dances, and it is speculated that there are currently more than 6,000 dance tunes, from jigs to reels to hornpipes currently in circulation in addition to slow airs, polkas and 'pieces' - a listening version of the jig.

Continued on P.70

Dennis Doody's

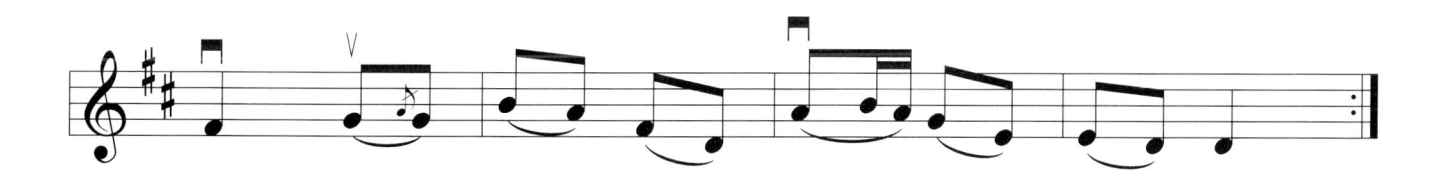

Ex. 108   Polka

O'Sullivan's Fancy

Ex. 109   Polka

Bakerswell Polka No. 1

I first heard the following polkas played by a group called Bakerswell. It was comprised of such great musicians as Seán Potts, Seán Óg Potts and Ronan Browne.

Ex. 110

Bakerswell Polka No. 2

Ex. 111

The Priest

Mary Willie's

This Is My Love Do You Like Her

Going To The Well For Water

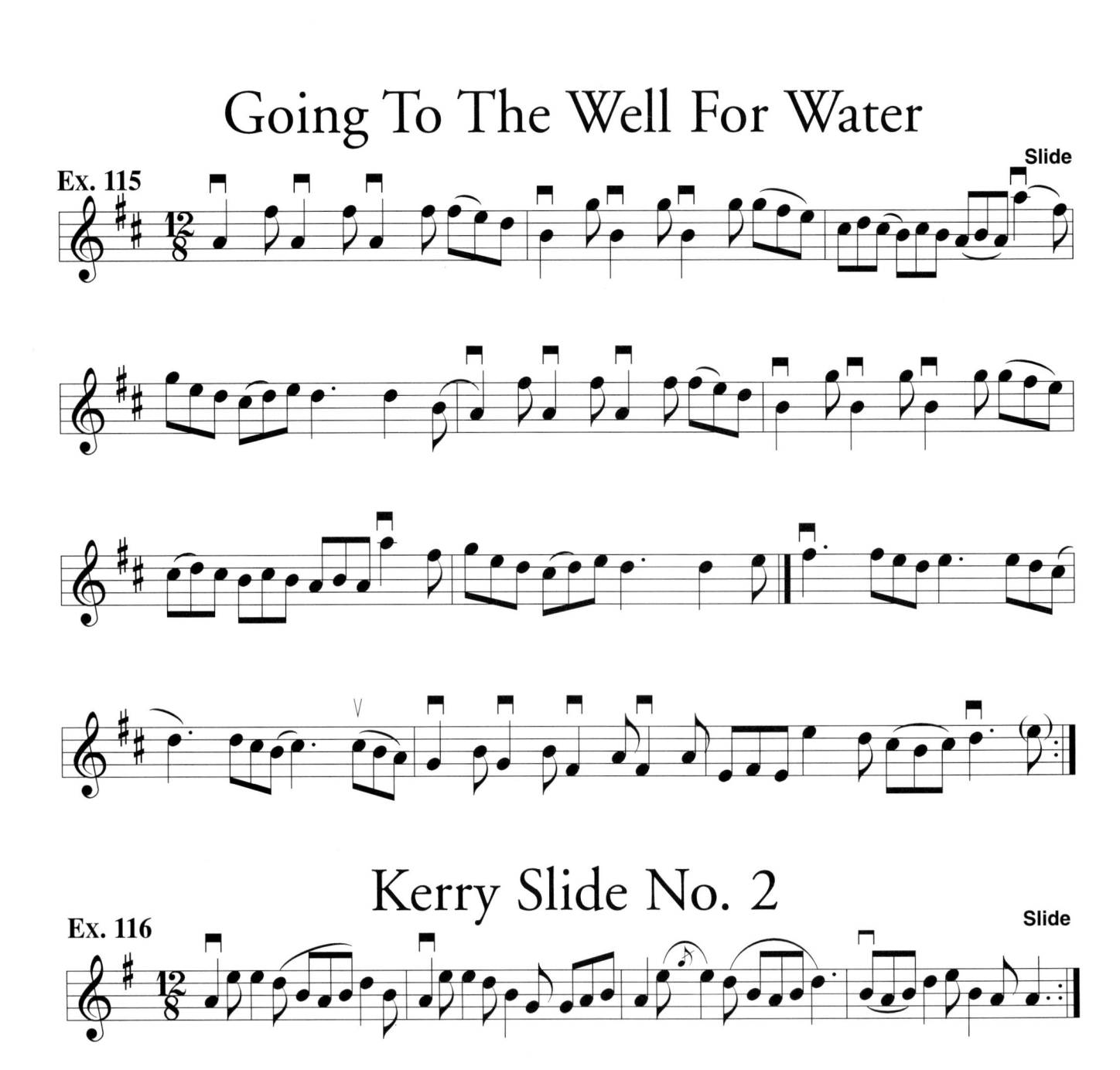

Ex. 115

Kerry Slide No. 2

Ex. 116

KEY POINTS

This section contains some of the more complex tunes in the book. Work through them slowly, as they will take much experience to play properly. This is especially true with slow airs.

Reels are the most popular of traditional tunes, but remember they don't have to be played fast. Keep the pace steady and to your own standard.

By now you will have become aware of some of the more refined aspects of the music itself, such as phrasing, the need to learn music from many sources, and the effect bowing can have on rhythm.

Reels

Reels are without doubt the most popular type of tune played in Irish music. The time signature is 4/4 (common time), sometimes indicated by a C sign replacing 4/4. Although this time signature tells us that there are four crotchet beats in each bar, a bar of a reel often contains eight quavers.

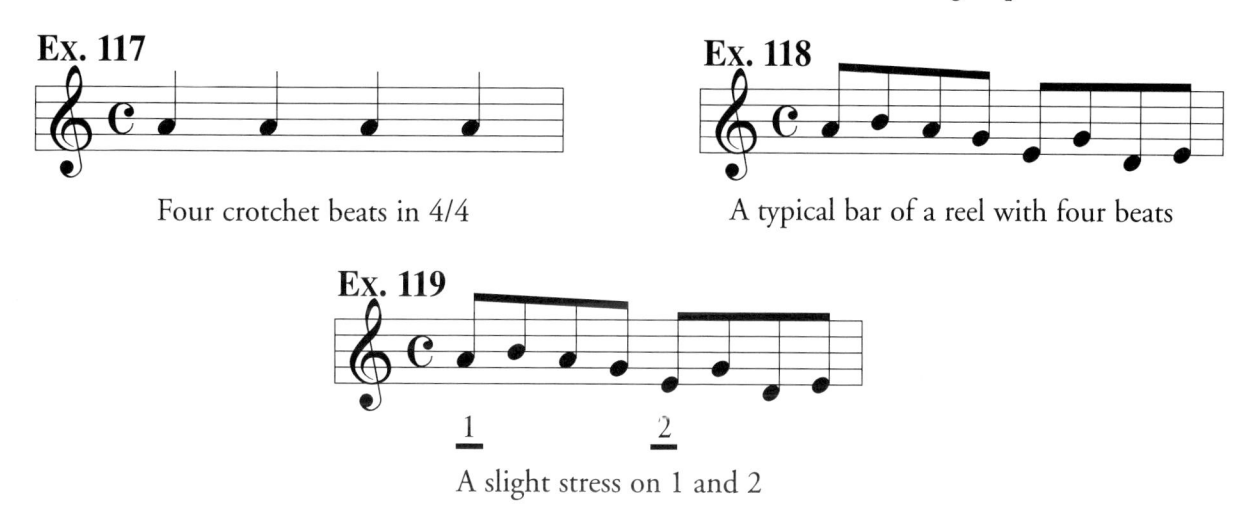

Ex. 117

Four crotchet beats in 4/4

Ex. 118

A typical bar of a reel with four beats

Ex. 119

A slight stress on 1 and 2

Most players would count as in the above example and tap their feet at these points.
Ornamentation such as roll, triplets, etc. can alter the bar structure, and we will discuss these later.

O'Connell's Trip To Parliament

Here is a nice simple reel to begin with in the key of D. Ignore the bowing indicated until you have each note clear and the timing right.

Ex. 120   Reel

Bar 2 of the second part could also be written as at left, with B C# D treated as a slurred triplet.

Note: Reels are known as singles when each section of the tune has 4 bars rather than 8.

Jackie Coleman's

Slur all the triplets in the second part and use the fourth finger on the A string instead of crossing to the E string for the triplet in the first, second and fifth bars of the second part.

Ex. 121   Reel

Styles of Playing – Continued

The jig is probably the oldest form of dance music surviving and is found in three forms, the single, the double and the slip jig. Though there has been a suggestion of an Italian origin to the jig (mostly associated with the titles of O'Carolan's tunes) reference suggest that there were jigs in existence before the mid 17th century. Whatever the origin, most existing jigs are at least melodically Irish in origin. The most poplar ones today have been composed by fiddlers and pipers of the 18th and 19th century, though these may have ben derived from older marches and songs. Curiously, tunes similar to jigs were in circulation in England before O'Carolan, but very few were found among the Scots. The reel is a more recent addition and undoubtedly originated in Scotland. Reels are amongst the most popular tunes for dancing and most in currency at present are thought to date from the mid 18th century.

Most common ones, in fact, have been attributed to known Scottish composers, but have been popular in Ireland for so long that they have become naturalised., like "Miss McLeod's", "Rakish Paddy" and "Lucy Campbell". The hornpipe is similar but has a more defined accent on the first and third beats of each bar. The hornpipe is considered to be English in origin. Purely instrumental music played today takes two common forms, the 'piece' version of the double or single jig, and the slow air. A 'piece' involves filling in intervals in the original jigs with ornamentation and embellishments. These pieces are often rather long and descriptive, with a multitude of sound effects that tell a tale.

Continued on P.75

Joe Cooley's Reel

'Cooley's' and 'The Wise Maid' were made famous by Joe Cooley, the great box player from Galway. Both tunes are more suited to the box and can be difficult to master on the fiddle, but the rich melody and rhythm is hard to find in many recent compositions. In the second piece, watch for the C natural in the fourth bar of the second part.

Ex. 122   Reel

The Wise Maid

Ex. 123   Reel

Jenny's Chickens

When this tune was recorded by Michael Coleman in 1934 it became a standard version and a classic to which many fiddlers aspired. Each time round, Coleman would vary the tune, making it difficult for the listener to obtain a proper version! Go over the tune in two or four bar phrases to get the ornamentation clear and watch for the cross bowing in the last part. The key signature is B minor, so all G's are played sharp.

Ex. 124   **Reel**

The Morning Dew

This tune uses extensive first finger cross-bowing in the second and third part. Practise very slowly at first, and play one bow per note until you are happy that you have a good clean sound on each note.

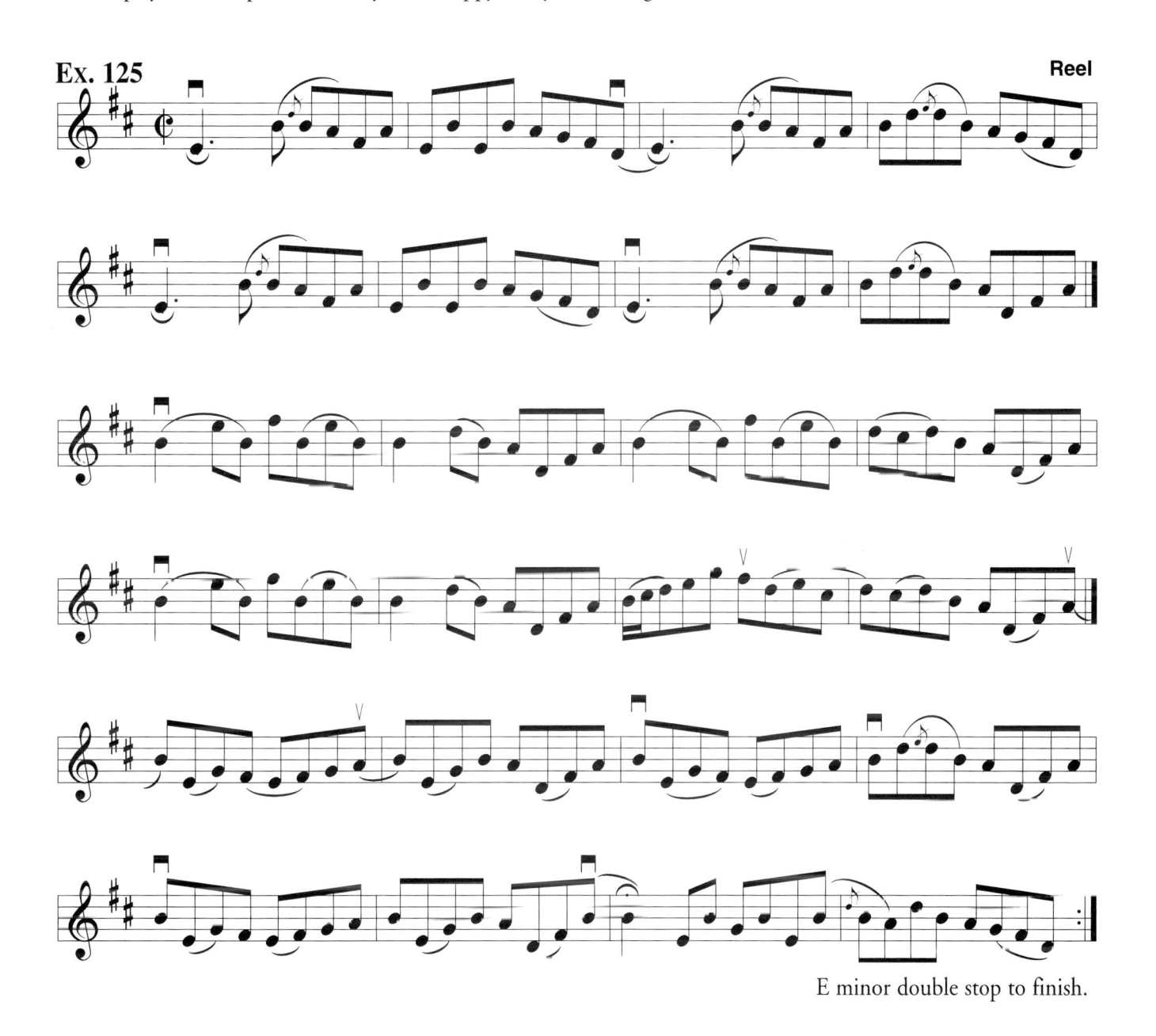

Ex. 125
Reel

E minor double stop to finish.

The Pigeon On The Gate

This reel in the key of E minor is popular on both fiddle and accordion. Many versions of the tune exist depending on the instrument on which it is played. As below, bars can be embellished or varied to suit the player's preference for short rolls or triplets. Slur the triplets in bar 3 of the first part and in bars 2, 6 and 7 of the second part.

Ex. 126 Reel

Ex. 127 can replace bars 3 and 4 of the second part as a variation.

Ex. 128 can replace bars 5 and 6 of the first part as a variation.

Advanced Ornamentation

This section involves ornamentation that requires an intermediate playing level and a good grasp of triplets, rolls, etc. Two or more ornaments can be used in conjunction with each other – such as a sliding roll, which brings us to our next point.

Sliding

Sliding is one of the more expressive aspects of traditional fiddling. To perform a slide, a string must be continually bowed whilst a finger moves up the fingerboard, changing the pitch. The slide generally consists of a semitone (or less) change in pitch.

For a slide to be most effective, a space in the tune must become available. To play a slide, the finger is brought back (toward the nut) roughly a centimetre and pushed gently up the string while pressed on the fingerboard.

Example:
An arrow in front of the note indicates a slide. (Here in the reel 'The Morning Star'.)

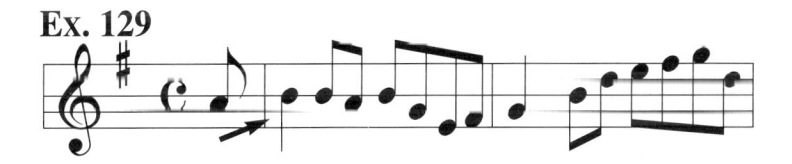

Ex. 129

Ex. 130

A slide in the jig 'Banish Misfortune'

When playing a slide, be careful not to bring your finger beyond the desired position. The slide is generally played over a dotted crotchet or shorter note, and the left hand does not move when playing the slide, only the finger. Finally, the slide is not an essential piece of ornamentation, so listen to some regional playing styles and see if you would like to use it.

> ### Styles of Playing – Continued
>
> *A good example is the "Battle of Aughrim" which musically weaves the sounds of war, from the assemble of troops for battle and the frenzy of the fight to the laments over the slain. In the happier "Fox Chase", hounds, horns, horses and the general hullabaloo of the hunt conjoin for a special conclusion.*
>
> *The slow air could actually match the mythological category of the goltraí or weeping music and the main part of those played today are considered to be either original contemporary compositions or derived from written rather than traditional sources.*
>
> *According to legend, the kingship of Ireland was once held by two brothers (Eremon and Eber), one of whom took residence in the south and one in the north. Before the two parted ways, however, they cast lots upon their artists to see which each should take. The poet, 'learned man or mighty power' went north towards 'dignity and learning', while the harper went south towards 'strings sweetness of music'.*

Continued on P.82

Cross-Bowing

In many traditional pieces the melody repeats alternately from one string to another. Traditional fiddlers use a distinctive rocking pattern which improves slurring across two strings. This is known as crossbowing.

Ex. 131

Here is cross-bowing in the second bar of the second part of 'The Wheels of the World'. The second finger must be placed on the A and E strings while the hand rocks from one string to another.

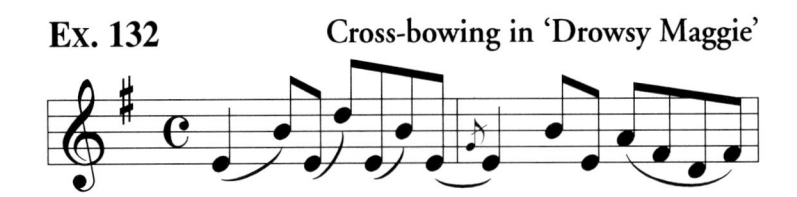

Ex. 132 Cross-bowing in 'Drowsy Maggie'

The cross-bowing here is quite complex and will need a lot of practice to play smoothly. Two E's are separated by a grace note run over the bar line. By running the bow through a bar line, the rhythm appears less obvious and helps the melody sing out.

Cross-bowing can be done in many ways often depending on the structure of the bars. The more notes you slur the more difficult the bowing becomes. Plenty of separate practice is needed for these examples.

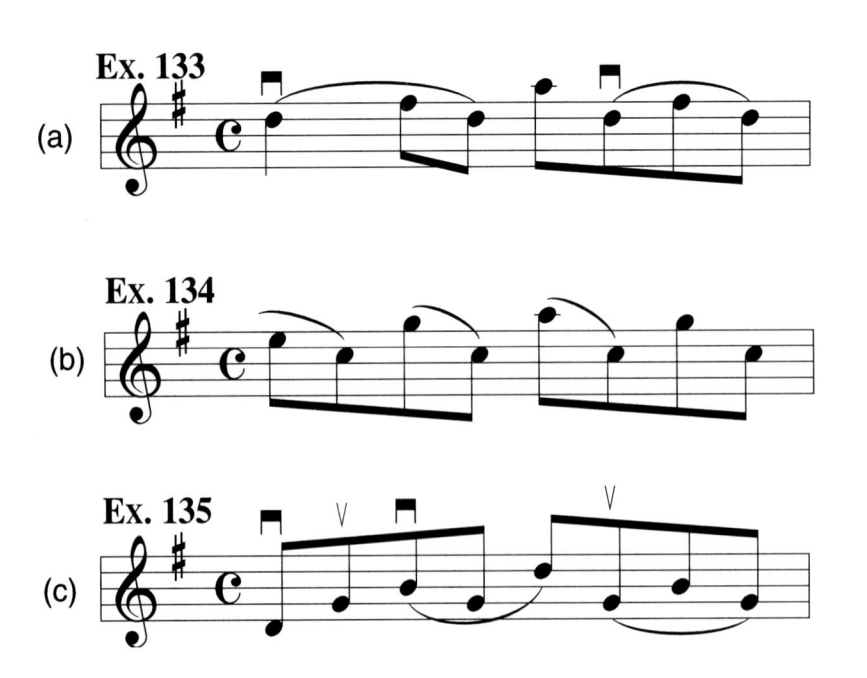

(a) **Ex. 133**

(b) **Ex. 134**

(c) **Ex. 135**

In example (a) crossbowing using the third finger. In example (b) second finger cross-bowing going from C natural to G natural sounds particularly nice on the fiddle. Example (c) indicates bowing across the beat in the bar and sounds less rigid than (a) or (b). Look for more examples in the reels section.

Double Stopping

Double stopping is when two strings are bowed as one to give an effect of playing a chord. There are two places where double stopping can be used: within a tune to complement the melody and at the very end of a tune.

Here are examples in a jig and a reel. **N.B.:** A note written directly above a note means that the two must be played simultaneously.

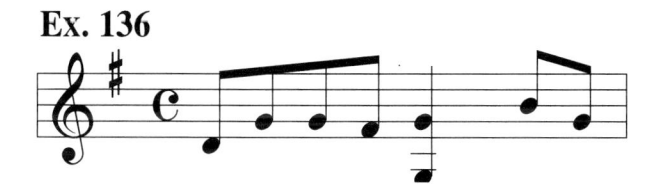

Ex. 136

Ex. 137

Double stopping in 'The Red Haired Lass'   A double stop in 'Garret Barry's Jig'

It is important to note that double stops are not randomly inserted into a tune. By playing and listening carefully to other players you will soon get the idea of where to put them.

Here is another example at the end of a tune:

Ex. 138

A chord at the end of 'Rakish Paddy'

Here is a scale which involves playing two strings for each stroke, good practice for droning also (see next section). Avoid a scratchy sound; try to get a constant sound from each chord. Use a third of the bow for each stroke.

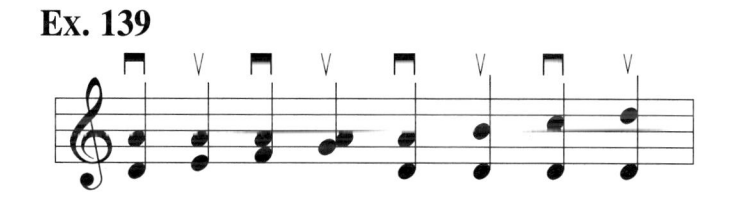

Ex. 139

Droning

Droning is achieved when another string is played with the original string to complement the melody, acting as sort of bass note accompaniment. To play the drone, the bow is drawn across two strings simultaneously while one is played open. Here is an example of droning in the first part of 'Stenson's Reel'. The drone covers three bars, with a possibility of a slight break on the last note of the second bar. To create it hold your 4th finger on the D string at the note A and bow the D and A strings together

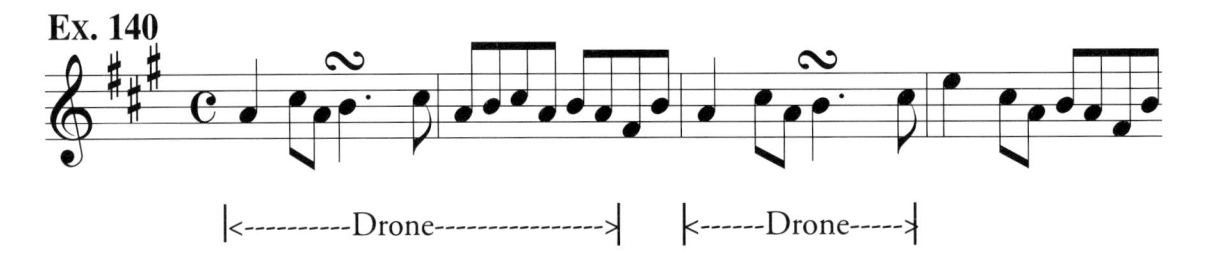

Ex. 140

|<----------Drone---------------->| |<------Drone----->|

The playing of the drone often involves the string to the left of the main one; this may be played open, or the fourth finger may be used on the string (as above) to create the same note.

Practise scales playing open string notes with the fourth finger to build up the strength and accuracy needed.

Trebling

A triplet whose three notes are of the same pitch and are bowed separately is known as a treble When trebling, the emphasis is on the rhythm created rather than on the notes being played. A small number of fiddlers employ what they call a **double treble**, a group of five separately bowed notes. It is very difficult to perform, requiring a double flick of the bow hand. It is generally restricted to hornpipes or slow reels.

Ex. 141

Treble

Ex. 142

Double Treble

The starting bow direction of a treble or double treble is totally up to the individual.

Trebling is sometimes done in jigs also; in this example it emphasises a solid off-beat rhythm.

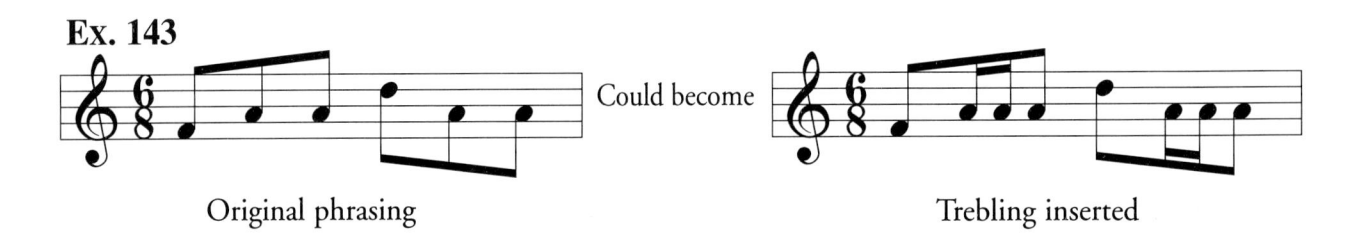

Ex. 143

Original phrasing   Could become   Trebling inserted

Miscellaneous tunes

A collection of over thirty tunes is now presented. It includes reels, jigs, hornpipes, slides, polkas, set dances and airs. Most are popular fiddle tunes and are in continuous articulation throughout the country. The ornamentation in this section is left to the discretion of the player.

The Humours of Kilkenny	The Little Stack of Barley
The High Part of the Road	Sliabh na mBan
Drops of Spring Water	Chief O'Neill's Favourite
The Cameronian	The Kesh Jig
Christmas Eve	Carolan's Draught
Siobhán Hurls	The Bucks of Oranmore
The Star Above the Garter	Drowsy Maggie
Con Thadhgo's	East of Glendart
The Roundabout	Apples in Winter
The Otter's Holt	Tatter Jack Walsh
The Connaught Man's Rambles	Tell Her I Am
When You're Sick is it Tea You Want?	The Mountain Road
The Knocknaboul	St. Anne's Reel
The Job of Journeywork	An Phis Fliuch
The Star of Munster	Hardiman the Fiddler
Rakish Paddy	The Ace and Deuce of Pipering
The Hare's Paw	The Rights of Man
Sonny Murray's	The Rose in the Heather
The Tap Room Reel	The Coach Road to Sligo
Táimse im Chodladh	

The Humours of Kilkenny

Ex. 144   *Slip Jig*

The High Part of the Road

Ex. 145   *Jig*

Drops of Spring Water

Ex. 146

Slip Jig

The Cameronian

Ex. 147

Reel

Christmas Eve

Ex. 148   Reel

Styles of Playing – Continued

Though of course fine traditional music is found all over Ireland, there are distinct characteristics between Northern and Southern fiddle styles. Northern playing is distinguished by active, single strokes and a minimum of ornamentation, whereas in the South, rolling (the grouping together of three grace notes) and embellishing (filling in intervals) is typical. All irish music, however, is essentially melodic: that is, relying on ornamentation rather than harmony, accompaniment or modulation.

Continued on P.86

Siobhán Hurls

Ex. 149 — Slide

The Star Above the Garter

Ex. 150 — Slide

Con Thadhgo's

Ex. 151 — Polka

The Roundabout

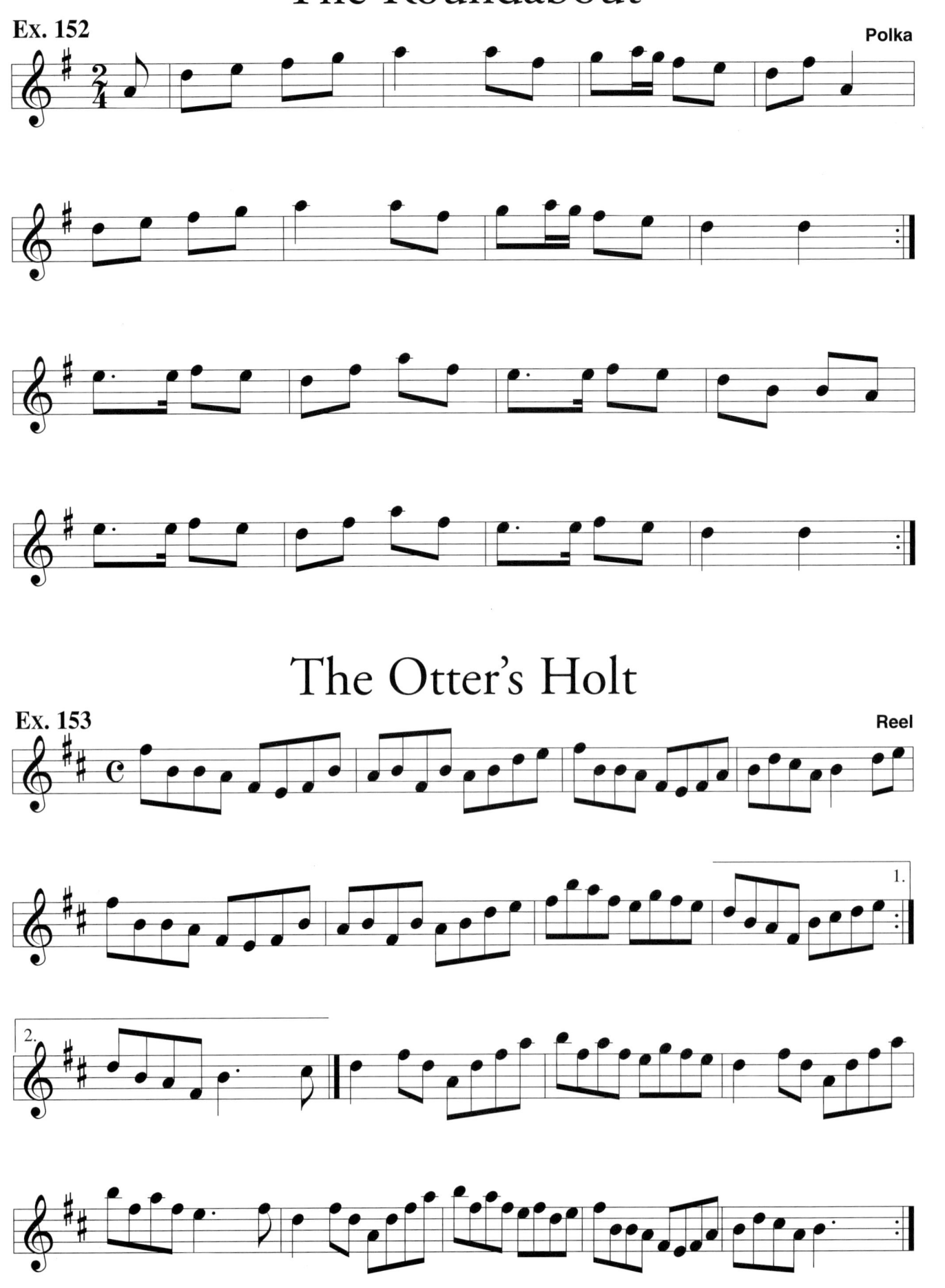

Ex. 152

Polka

The Otter's Holt

Ex. 153

Reel

The Connaughtman's Rambles

Ex. 154
Jig

When Sick, Is It Tea You Want?

Ex. 155
Jig

The Knocknaboul

Ex. 156   Polka

DOCUMENTATION

The first written collection of Irish music appeared in 1762, containing 49 airs and published by Neale Brothers in Dublin. Only one copy survives and it is preserved among the collections of Edward Bunting at Queens University, Belfast. The Neale Brothers also published a collection of O'Carolan's airs while O'Carolan was still alive.

    But it was not until the late part of that century that first hand notations of Irish music were taken down directly from traditional players such as Edward Bunting's collections of Ancient Irish Music.

Bunting had displayed a unique musical aptitude at an early age and by the time he was 19 was asked to be scribe for the Belfast Festival of 1792. Afterwards Bunting took a great interest in music and travelled widely seeking out music through the North of Ireland and Connaught. His 1796 volume contains 66 airs. The Society for the Preservation and Publication of Melodies of Ireland was the first official organisation to concern itself with Irish music and was founded in 1851 by the Scots-Irishman George Petrie.

The Job of Journeywork

Ex. 157   **Set Dance**

Documentation - continued

A manuscript containing 2,148 pieces was eventually published in the first decade of this century. Unfortunately the early collections of Irish music are not totally reliable as the collectors came largely from outside the tradition and often unwittingly submitted the music to their own notions of correct harmony which were foreign to Irish music.

The best collectors of Irish music were those who not only played the music themselves but spoke Irish as well, attuning them to the peculiarities of the Irish vocal tradition which had subtle similarities with the instrumental music. One such man was James Goodman from Ventry who collected a wealth of material in Co.Kerry between 1860 and 1866. The finest collection of Irish dance music, however, was made by Chicago Chief Superintendant of Police Francis O'Neill, originally a native of Cork. O'Neill had a huge mental collection of tunes but was unable to commit them to paper - this aspect of the collection was done by his colleague James O'Neill.

Continued on P.96

The Star of Munster

Ex. 158 Reel

Rakish Paddy

Ex. 159 Reel

The Hare's Paw

Ex. 160   **Reel**

Sonny Murray's

Ex. 161   **Hornpipe**

The Tap Room

Ex. 162 *Reel*

The Little Stack of Barley

Ex. 163 *Hornpipe*

Sliabh na mBan

Ex. 164
Slow Air

Chief O'Neill's Favourite

Ex. 165

The Kesh Jig

Ex. 166

Carolan's Draught

O'Carolan

Ex. 167

The Bucks of Oranmore

Ex. 168

Reel

Drowsy Maggie

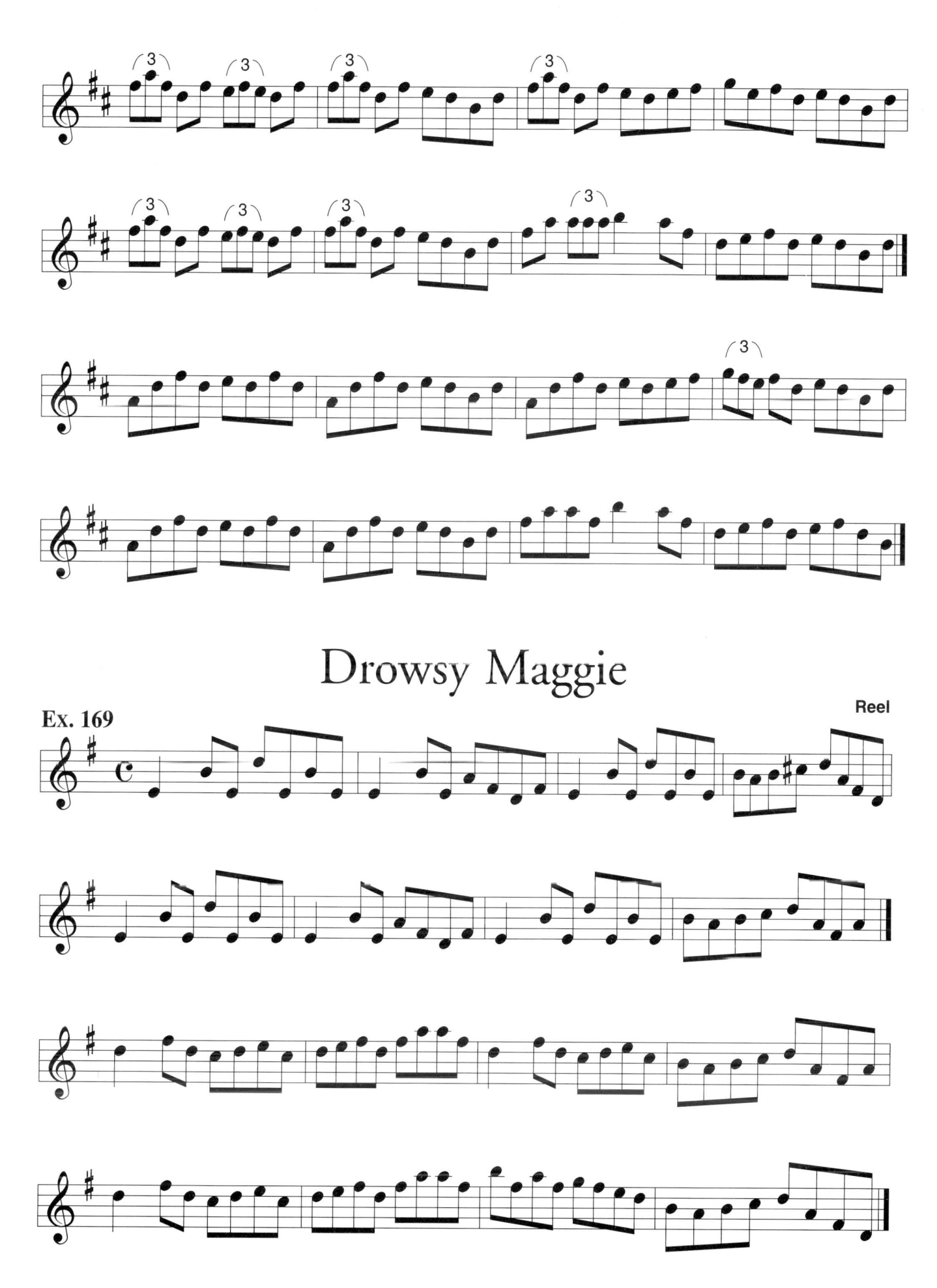

Reel

Ex. 169

East of Glendart

Ex. 170   Jig

Documentation - continued

The written collection of 1850 pieces appeared in 1903 and was the largest ever published. Of that vast number, 1,100 were dance tunes, and the O'Neill collection still enjoys wide circulation today.
Irish tunes are still in the process of evolution and new tunes are currently being written, which feature influences from all over the world. Hence the job of the collector will never be a static one, as cultural cross-fertilisation increases with human mobility. Without a doubt, however, the best way to understand Irish music is to learn to play, for the peculiarities of this rich tradition can never be understood from books or ear alone.

Molly McAnailly Burke

Apples in Winter

Ex. 171

Jig

Tatter Jack Walsh

Ex. 172

Jig

Tell Her I Am

Ex. 173 *Jig*

The Mountain Road

Ex. 174

Reel

St Anne's Reel

Ex. 175

Reel

An Phis Fliuch

Ex. 176

Slip Jig

Hardiman the Fiddler

Ex. 177

Slip Jig

The Ace and Deuce of Pipering

Ex. 178

Set Dance

The Rights of Man

Ex. 179 *Hornpipe*

The Rose in the Heather

Ex. 180 *Jig*

The Coach Road to Sligo

Ex. 181

Jig

Táimse im Chodladh

Ex. 182

Slow Air

Appendix I

STRINGS

Almost all traditional fiddlers use steel strings. Generally louder than gut or nylon, they respond better to heavy bow pressure. I have found these string brands nice to play on while being in a competitive price range: Dr Thomastik, Spirocore and Dominant. Give new strings time to settle; they will go flat for a while and affect overall tuning. Strings can be cleaned with a damp cloth (mixed with soap), rubbed down and dried off. When a string starts to lose its outer coil or if the pitch drops very quickly after playing an open string, it's time to change it. It may take some experience to notice this.

THE BOW AND RE-HAIRING

Bow hairs break when the hair touches the wood and stretches. When or if one does break, it is better to cut or bite the hair at one end, so as not to dislodge the others. Much of the hair used in Europe comes from China and Asia but Argentinian, English or Mongolian are also used. Stallion hair is probably the strongest and best hair to use. It is true that black hair is coarser, but any hair is better without being bleached. The average bow has roughly 150-200 hairs, depending on the thickness of the hair. A re-hair should cost in the region of £25. Finally, make sure to keep the bow hair immaculately clean.
I would recommend Hidersine or A.B. rosin as an alternative to rosin included with lower priced fiddle packages.

CLEANING THE FIDDLE

The fiddle itself should be cleaned quite regularly, especially the body between the fingerboard and the base of the bridge. Rosin can build up and eat into the wood eventually. A soft dry cloth should suffice to clean around this area.
Proper cleaning fluids for the whole of the fiddle are available;
I would recommend Gewa or Hildersol, both being particularly effective.

Discography

This discography indicates many of the important and influential players of this century. At the end there are some compilations that feature fiddle performances in duets and other settings.

Musician(s)	Title	Reference No.
Burke, Kevin	Up Close	Green Linnet SIF1052
Byrne, James	The Road To Glenlough	Claddagh CC52CD
Carroll, Liz	A Friend Indeed	Shanachie 34013
Carroll, Liz with Daithí Sproule	Liz Carroll	Green Linnet GL1092
Casey, Bobby	Casey In The Cowhouse	Bellbridge Records 001
Casey, Nollaig & Arty McGlynn	Lead The Knave	Round Tower MCGCD1
Carty, John	Last Night's Fun	Shanachie 79098
Coleman, Michael	Michael Coleman 1891-1945 The Classic Recordings of Michael Coleman The Legacy Of Michael Coleman	Gael Linn CECFD161 Shanachie 29002 Shanachie 33002
Connolly, Seamus	Notes From My Mind Here And There	Green Linnet GLCD1087 Green Linnet GLCD1098
Creagh, Séamus	Came The Dawn	PIPCD 7330
Crannitch, Matt	Éistigh Seal	Gael Linn CEF 104
Custy, Mary with Eoin O'Neill	With A Lot Of Help From Their Friends	GLCD 3077
Doherty, John	Bundle And Go Johnny Doherty	Gael Linn CEF 072/073 CBE 002
Doherty, Mickey	Gravel Walks	Shanachie 34009
Gavin, Frankie	Frankie Gavin & Alec Finn Irlande Frankie Goes To Town (and anything by De Danann)	Ocora C560021 Green Linnet GL 3051 Topic 12T364
Gillespie, Hugh	Classic Recordings Of Irish Traditional Fiddle Music	Green Linnet GLCD3066
Glackin, Paddy	Glackin In Full Spate	Gael Linn CEF 060 Gael Linn CEFC 153
Hayden, Cathal	Handed Down	Rainbow RBA 116
Hayes, Martin	Martin Hayes Under The Moon	Green Linnet GLCD 1127 Green Linnet GLCD 1155
Ivers, Eileen	Fresh Takes (with John Whelan)	Green Linnet GLCD 1075
Keane, Seán Keane, Seán	Gusty's Frolics Jig It In Style	Claddagh CC17 Claddagh CCF 25CD
Kelly, James	The Ring Sessions (with Zan McLeod) Capell Street	SPINC 999 Bowhand Records 0001
Kelly, John Jnr and James	John and James Kelly	Tara 1008, PTICD 1005

Killoran, Paddy	Paddy Killoran's Back In Town	Shanachie 33003
Lennon, Charlie	Deora an Deoraí	Gael Linn CEF 112
	Musical Memories	WOM 101
McGann, Andy	It's A Hard Road To Travel (with Paul Brady)	Shanachie 34011
McGlinchey, Brendan	Music Of A Champion	Silverhill PSH 100
McGuire, Seán	Champion Of Champions	PTICD 1005
	The Best Of Seán Maguire	COX 1006
	Ireland's Champion Fiddler	SOLP 1031
Milne, Vincent	A Small Island	Ossian OSS 70
Mulvihill, Brendan	The Flax In Bloom	Green Linnet GLCD 1020
Mulvihill, Martin	Traditional Irish Fiddling From County Limerick	Green Linnet GLCD1012
Murphy, Dennis	Music From Sliabh Luchra Fiddle Master	RTÉ 174 CD
Morrison, James	The Pure Genius Of James Morrison	Shanachie 33004
	The Professor (2 cassettes)	Viva Voce 001
O'Keeffe, Padraig	The Sliabh Luchra Fiddle Master	RTÉ 174 CD
Peoples, Tommy	Tommy Peoples	Comhaltas CL13
	The High Part Of The Road (with Paul Brady)	Shanachie 34007
	The Iron Man (with Daithí Sproule)	Shanachie 79044
Potts, Tommy	The Liffey Banks	Cladagh CC13
Reavey, Ed	Ed Reavey	Rounder 6008
Smyth, Séan	The Blue Fiddle	Lun CD 060
Thompson, Séamus	Longford's Own	GTD Heritage HC094

Duets

Burke, Kevin with Jackie Daly	Eavesdropper	LUN CD 3039
Canny, Paddy with P.J. Hayes	All Ireland Champions	Dublin DU-LP 1003
Carroll, Liz with Tommy Maguire	Kiss me Kate	Shanachie 29010
Carroll, Liz with Billy McComiskey & Daithí Sproule	Trian	Flying Fish FF705068
Creagh, Séamus with Jackie Daly	Séamus Creagh with Jackie Daly	Gael Linn CEFCD057
Gavin, Frankie & Paul Brock	Ómos do Joe Cooley	Gael Linn CEFCD115
Glackin, Kevin & Séamus	Na Saighdiurí - Northern Lights	Gael Linn CEFCD140
Glackin, Paddy with Jolyon Jackson	Hidden Ground	Tara 2009
Kelly, James with Paddy O'Brien & Daithí Sproule	James Kelly with Paddy O'Brien & Daithí Sproule	Shanachie 34014
	Spring In The Air	Shanachie 29018
Linnane, Tony with Noel Hill	Tony Linnane and Noel Hill	Tara 2006
McGann, Andy with Paddy Reynolds	Andy McGann with Paddy Reynolds	Shanachie 34008

McGuire, Séamus & Manus	The Humours Of Lissadell	Folk Legacy FSE78
	Carousel (with Daithí Sproule)	Gael Linn CEFCD105
	The First Month Of Summer	Green Linnet GLCD1079
Murphy, Dennis & Julia Clifford	The Star Above The Garter	Claddagh CC5CD

Compilations

An Fhidil 1	Gael Linn CEF 068
An Fhidil 2	Gael Linn CEF 069
Ceol an Chláir	Comhaltas CL 17
'Dear Old Erin's Isle', Irish Traditional Music From America (includes Brendan Mulvihill, Liz Carroll, Kevin Burke, Eileen Ivers, etc.)	Nimbus NI5350
Fiddlesticks: Irish Traditional Music From Donegal (includes Tommy Peoples, Ciarán Tourish, Dermot McLoughlin, etc.)	Nimbus 5350
Milestone At The Garden: Irish Fiddle Masters (includes James Morrison, Hugh Gillespie, Denis Murphy, Ed Reavey, etc.)	Rounder CD 1123
My Love Is In America: Irish Traditional Music From America (includes Martin Hayes, Séamus Connolly, Andy McGann, etc.)	Green Linnet GLCD1110
Playing With Fire The Celtic Fiddle Collection (inc. Seán Keane, Kevin Burke, etc.)	Green Linnet GLCD1101
The Donegal Fiddle (Various)	RTE CD196

Festivals And Events

At the time of writing, most of the festival and events listed below have been running for several years. They are an ideal opportunity for you to look at and listen to accomplished musicians – and perhaps to join in the session yourself.

MARCH   Feis Cheoil, RDS, Merrion Road, Dublin. (Between 3rd and 4th Weekends).

MAY   Fleadh Nua, Ennis, Co. Clare. (3rd Weekend).

JUNE   Denis Murphy Memorial Weekend, Knocknagree, Mallow, Co. Cork

Byrne/Perry Summer School, Gorey, Co. Wexford. (1st Weekend)

JULY   Willie Clancy Summer School, Milltown Malbay, Co. Clare (First weekend in July). This includes numerous pub sessions, concerts and workshops by some of Ireland's greatest musicians. (Between 1st and 2nd Weekend)

South Sligo Summer School, Tubbercurry, Co. Sligo. (Between 2nd and 3rd Weekends).
Kilfenora Music School, Co. Clare. (Between 2nd and 3rd Weekends).

Joe Mooney Summer School, Co. Leitrim.(Between 2nd and 3rd Weekends).

Galway Arts Festival, Galway City. (Between 3rd and 4th Weekends).

James Morrison Traditional Weekend, Riverstown, Co. Sligo.

Phil Murphy Weekend, Carrick-on-Bannow, Co. Wexford. (Last Weeekend)

AUGUST   Ballyshannon Folk Festival, Ballyshannon, Co. Donegal. (1st Weekend)

O'Carolan Harp Festival, Keadue, Co. Roscommon. (1st Weekend)

Scoil Shamhraidh d'Fhidleireachta Thir Chonaill / Donegal Fiddlers Summer School, Glencolumbkille, Co. Donegal.

Feakle Traditional Music Festival, Feakle, Co. Clare. (2nd Weekend)
This region is steeped in musical richness, with people like Martin Hayes, P.J. Hayes, Martin Rochford, Vincent Griffin and Paddy Canny living in the area. The programme includes music, singing sessions and a gala concert.

Aonach Paddy O'Brien, Nenagh, Co. Tipperary. (3rd Week)

Coleman County Traditional Festival, Gurteen, Co. Sligo. (Last Weekend)

AUGUST	Fleadh Cheoil na hÉireann. The venue for the All-Ireland Fleadh can change annually. Full details are available from Comhaltas Ceolteóirí Éireann, Baile na Monach, Co. Baile Atha Cliath, Ph. (01) 280 0295. (Last Weekend)
	Féile Mhic Andáin - Thomastown traditional music festival - August Bank Holiday Weekend. (1st Weekend)
OCTOBER	Joe Cooley Weekend, Gort, Co. Galway. (Last Weekend)
NOVEMBER	Ennis Traditional Festival, Ennis, Co. Clare. (2nd Weekend)
DECEMBER	Scoil Gheimhridh Frankie Kennedy, Bunbeg, Co. Donegal. (Last Weekend)

Bibliography

Ceol Rince na hÉireann, Vols. 1,2,3 & 4 by Breathnach, Brendan,	Irish Govt. Pub., Dublin.
The Roche Collection of Irish Music	Ossian Pub.
O'Neill's Music of Ireland 1001 Melodies	Walton's, Dublin.
O'Neill's Music of Ireland 1850 Melodies	Dan Collins, New York.
O'Neill's Music of Ireland Over 1000 Fiddle Tunes	Miles Krassen, Oak Pub.
The Collected Compositions of Ed Reavy	J.M. Reavy, Green Grass Music.
Trip to Sligo, Flaharty, Bernard,	Bernard Flaharty, 1990.
Musical Memories by Charlie Lennon	Worldmusic Publications.

Further Reading

Bowing Styles in Irish Fiddle Playing (Vol.1) by David Lyth, Comhaltas Ceoltóirí Éireann 1981
Bowing Styles in Irish Fiddle Playing (Vol.2) by David Lyth, Comhaltas Ceoltóirí Éireann 1997

Traditional Music in Ireland, Tomás Ó Canainn, Routledge & Keegan Paul, London

A Trip to Sligo, A Guide to the Sligo Style, Tony de Marco and Miles Krassen, Silver Spear Publications, Pittsburgh, Pennsylvania.

Irish Music Magazine, published by Marne Ltd., P.O. Box 25, Bray, Co. Wicklow.